Essential

Iceland

by
DAVID WILLIAMS

1,000 krona = $15

PASSPORT BOOKS
a division of *NTC Publishing Group*
Lincolnwood, Illinois USA

Published by Passport Books, a division of NTC Publishing Group, 4255 West Touhy Avenue, Lincolnwood (Chicago), Illinois 60646–1975 U.S.A.

The contents of this publication are believed correct at the time of printing. Nevertheless, the publishers cannot accept responsibility for errors or omissions, nor for changes in details given. We are always grateful to readers who let us know of any errors or omissions they come across, and future printings will be updated accordingly.

Published by Passport Books in conjunction with The Automobile Association of Great Britain.

Written by David Williams
"Peace and Quiet" section by Paul Sterry

Library of Congress Catalog
Card Number 93–85615
ISBN 0–8442–8915–9

10 9 8 7 6 5 4 3 2 1

PRINTED IN TRENTO, ITALY

Front cover picture: Eldgjá Ófaerufoss waterfall

The weather chart displayed on **page 96** of this book is calibrated in °C and millimetres. For conversion to °F and inches simply use the following formula:

$$25\cdot4mm = 1\ inch \qquad °F = 1\cdot8 \times °C + 32$$

CONTENTS

This book employs a
simple rating system to
help choose which
places to visit:

◆◆◆   do not miss

◆◆   see if you can

◆   worth seeing if
         you have time

INTRODUCTION

Of all the countries in the world, Iceland has
one of the greatest varieties of scenery within a
relatively small area. In an island just a little
larger than Ireland, there are active volcanoes,
geysers, cold deserts, massive ice-caps, glacial
lagoons with icebergs, and green valleys
complete with geothermally-heated
greenhouses.

It is an island of extremes. It sits at the junction
of the Old and the New Worlds and is being torn
apart as these two great continents drift slowly
across the Earth's surface. One-tenth of its
surface is covered with lavafields less than
10,000 years old and there are always threats of
eruptions that could spell disaster for this
otherwise tranquil country.

Iceland boasts Europe's greatest ice-cap, Vatnajökull, a huge mass that sends cold tongues of ice down the valleys, ripping up mountains on their way and dumping vast amounts of black sand by the coast. But if the dangers of fire and ice are not enough by themselves, there are even active volcanoes lurking deep below the ice-caps – subglacial eruptions can unleash so much pent-up energy that a massive torrent of water, with a rate of flow greater than that of the River Amazon, can tear glaciers apart and catastrophically alter the landscape.

This varied but not entirely inhospitable landscape offers favourable habitats to many birds. Millions of seabirds breed in the coastal areas, while the rather less numerous whimbrels, owls, and ptarmigan make their home in the high moorlands. Iceland has long been a haven for ornithologists, especially the district around Mývatn where tens of thousands of ducks gather during the breeding season. But you don't have to travel too far to see the birds – even Reykjavík's lake is home to swans, ducks, geese and arctic terns.

For visitors seeking the peace and quiet so lacking in today's world, the Icelandic countryside, with its vast open spaces and unique landscape, offers one of the world's few unspoilt corners. However, it is far from being an 'uncivilised' country devoid of creature-comforts, and visitors will soon discover one of the Icelanders' favourite pastimes – swimming or just lazing about in geothermally-heated swimming pools. Iceland in midsummer is also the place for the sun seeker; no, not for sunbathing, but for enjoying colourful sunsets well past midnight. You can even play golf through the night! There is also something for visitors who enjoy the hustle and bustle of city life, since Reykjavik, the world's most northerly capital, is a lively city with museums, galleries and parks to wander in – and all in a pollution-free environment too. Because the city's buildings are heated by natural hot water, there is no need for the smoke chimneys so common in other capitals.

This was the last inhabitable part of Europe to be colonised. In the 8th century, intrepid Viking seafarers from Scandinavia braved the North Atlantic in search of a new home. They found a land that was very different from anything they had ever seen before, but one in which they soon established a nation that aspired to great things. They founded colonies in Greenland and settled in North America, 500 years before Christopher Columbus set foot there. But their achievements were not just those of heroic travellers. Icelanders gave the world the Sagas, the tales of the Norsemen. These stories have stood the test of time and are now regarded as being amongst the greatest treasures of world literature. They also established their own national assembly, the Althing, which, against all odds, lasted for some eight centuries as the highest expression of the nation's will. Unhappily, the great achievements of these determined people were blighted by the forces of nature as eruptions played havoc with their lives. One 18th-century eruption killed about a quarter of the entire population. Plagues and crop failures periodically reduced the people to subsistence level and this was made worse by centuries of foreign domination – first under the Norwegian crown, and then the Danish. It was not until the 19th century that Icelanders began the struggle for independence and this goal was only achieved in the mid-20th century. For centuries Icelanders have fought against the twin difficulties of nature (in the form of volcanic eruptions) and foreign domination; today, they are a nation with a pride in their ability to prosper against all odds. Although there have been ups and downs in the economic life of the country since World War II, the Icelanders have managed to exploit the sea's rich harvest to the point where they now enjoy one of the highest standards of living in the world. The modern Icelander is justly proud of the nation's history and how its people have revolutionised their way of life this century. For all the outward appearances of being in step with today's 'high-tech' way of life, they have a deep sense of history that is more profound than most of the European nations – they have proven that the spirit of the early Viking explorers has been able to overcome all adversaries on this unique Atlantic island.

BACKGROUND

The landscape

Iceland: the volcanic island

For a long time Iceland has been regarded as something of a 'natural laboratory' for scientists trying to unravel the secrets of how nature builds (and changes) the surface of this planet. Indeed, Iceland's geological history has helped scientists piece together the secrets of how volcanoes work, how mountain chains are formed and even how continents and oceans are created and subsequently changed. Iceland might seem to be in rather an odd location, stuck in the middle of the northern reaches of the Atlantic and well away from the major landmasses, but its mid-ocean position is due entirely to its volcanic origin, as it is essentially a very prominent peak in the long mountain chain known as the Mid-Atlantic Ridge. This chain of mountains runs from the Arctic to the Antarctic and was formed by submarine volcanic activity; hence the string of volcanic islands in the Atlantic such as Jan Mayen Island, Iceland, the Azores, the Canary Islands, the Cape Verde Islands and Tristan da Cunha.

The earth's surface is thought to be made up of seven major 'plates' that 'float' on the surface.

The restless earth. In Iceland, the internal workings of the planet are revealed. Thermal springs, such as these at Krísuvík, are common

These plates are in constant motion, some of them sliding past each other, some colliding, others moving away from each other. Iceland lies at the junction of the American plate and the European and African plates, and as these move slowly away from each other (by a couple of centimetres each year), volcanic eruptions occur along their line of contact. Lava rises up to seal the crack opened up between the separating plates. Hence the volcanoes and the volcanic islands in the middle of the Atlantic. In places where continents collide, one continent dives under the other and in so doing produces mountains. For example, as India moves northwards and collides with China, this motion crumples up the land, lifting the Himalayas even higher.

Iceland's oldest rocks are 'only' about 16 million years old so it is a comparatively 'new' landmass. The Mid-Atlantic Ridge runs right through the country and the two halves of the island are in fact gradually moving apart, widening the island as the two halves follow the continents on either side of the Atlantic. Iceland's most active volcanic areas lie on the ridge and since the edges of the country were on the ridge a long time ago, this accounts for the fact that the eastern and western parts of the island are also of volcanic origin but no longer volcanically-active.

The land: a general description

Iceland is Europe's second largest island and with an area of about 40,000 square miles (103,00 sq km), it is about 25 per cent bigger in area than Ireland. Most of the underlying rock is dark basaltic lava, sheets of which were poured out by volcanoes over the last 16 million years. The uninhabited central portion of the country, often referred to as the 'interior' or the 'central highlands' is composed of a series of mountain ranges, with vast deserts of grey ash or lavafields lying between them.

The interior's deserts were formed by the valley glaciers flowing from the huge ice-caps that dominate the interior, the biggest of which are Vatnajökull, Langjökull and Hofsjökull. The glacial rivers flowing from these ice masses carry torrents of water down to the sea, with the

Volcanic vent at Mývatn. As well as having superb examples of very recent volcanic activity, the Mývatn area has the best variety of scenery in Iceland

most powerful rivers flowing to the southern and northern coasts.

It was only in 1974 that the Icelanders managed to complete construction of the ring road, the lifeline that runs right round the island. Most of the country's population lives close to this. The main centres of population are generally found where there is enough flat land for agriculture and industry (mainly in the southwest) or where harbours can be built conveniently near the fishing areas (Reykjanes and Snæfellsnes peninsulas, and the fiords of the east, north and northwest).

Volcanism

Iceland's volcanic character has produced many different features that will constantly excite and amaze visitors.

The most violent activities are the (rather infrequent) eruptions and few visitors will be lucky (?) enough to see one. The most active area in recent years has been near Mývatn, a lake in the northeast of the country. Nine eruptions have taken place there between 1975 and 1984. Like most Icelandic eruptions, these have occurred not from one circular crater (which would build a conical volcano), but from long fissures. Red-hot fountains of molten lava gush out of a series of parallel fissures, with the lava flowing over the land and forming lavafields. Mývatn's recent eruptions have produced a very fluid type of lava and when this cools it forms characteristic coils of 'ropey lava'. If the lava is viscous then it flows much more slowly downhill, with great blocks of the congealed lava tumbling over one another. Instead of lava rivers, the front edge of this type of lavaflow is a tall wall, and when it finally solidifies it forms jagged 'block lava'. Both of these types of lava are composed of basalt. Visitors to the geologically older parts of the country (that is, the east and the northwest) will see that the mountains are composed of great sheets of these lavas and that they have now weathered to form step-like features and long graceful scree slopes, the lower parts of which are grassy.

During the various stages of an eruption, the activity might become very violent, with huge explosions taking place. When this happens, great clouds of ash or pumice might be thrown high into the air and massive clouds of dust form columns many kilometres high, producing brilliant sunsets. But not all eruptions produce the grey/black basalt that is so common. Visitors to Landmannalaugar will be treated to highly-coloured scenery that owes its brilliance to the rock called rhyolite that has been created there.

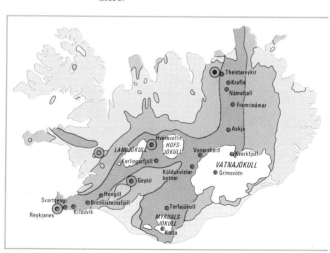

In many parts of the country, you can see interesting 'table mountains'. These are often composed of a rock known as palagonite, which is sometimes red or brown in colour. Table mountains were built by sub-glacial eruptions taking place deep below the surface of an ice-cap. As the eruption continued, the volcano grew and melted the ice, but in turn the volcano was constrained in extent by the ice and the chilling effect of the ice turned the rock into glassy fragments. Visitors to the northeast of the country will see fine table mountains such as Herdubreid, Búrfell and Bláfjall (the latter two are at Mývatn). A rather more uncommon type of volcano, a 'shield volcano', is formed by hundreds of small flows of very fluid lava cascading down from a central vent. Visitors to Thingvallavatn can see a superb example of this type of mountain called Skjaldbreidur.

The rocks beneath the earth's surface can remain warm for a long time after an eruption and often the groundwater that percolates down through the porous lava gets heated and turns into steam. The most spectacular result of this effect are the geysers, the most famous being Geysir and Strokkur in the southwest of the country; Strokkur regularly throws hot water

Below right: the geyser called Strokkur, Iceland's most spectacular since Geysir, the namesake of all geysers, ceased natural spurting

ICELAND : GEOLOGY

	Tertiary flood basalts · rocks older than 3 million years
	Quaternary flood basalts - rocks younger than 3 million years
	Bedrock covered by alluvial deposits and lava flows
	Neovolcanic zone - active zone of rifting and volcanism
	Main low temperature fields
	High temperature geothermal area
	Geysers

some 65 to 130 feet (20-40m) into the air. Many other places have small geysers where jets of very hot water a few centimetres high are continually erupting. These geysers have chemicals dissolved or suspended in their water and as the hot water flows away, these substances remain and can form plates of silicates around the vents, often producing intricate patterns.

In some districts, such as Mývatn and Krísuvík, hot water has mixed with blue/grey mud to form hot bubbling mudpools. Some of these can be quite enormous (several metres in diameter) while others spit out globules of mud which gradually build up a 'spatter cone'. Other manifestations of heat and volcanic liquids and gases rising earthwards are small vents encrusted with yellow sulphur or white gypsum, patches of different-coloured clays and warm springs that trickle slowly into lakes. One lake is so well supplied with these springs that it has the name Laugarvatn ('warm lake').

While all these volcanic features are of great fascination to visitors, the Icelanders have put nature's gift of geothermal energy to practical use. In many parts of the country, boreholes drilled deep into the rock allow steam and water to be tapped. This provides copious amounts of water for heating houses, schools, offices and public buildings. Indeed, many district schools, where children board during term-time, are built specifically where they can take advantage of hot water supplies. Often the hot water smells a little sulphurous, an unusual but not unpleasant smell. In some districts, notably in the southwest (Hveragerdi, for instance) and the west, the hot water is also used to heat glasshouses, allowing fresh fruit and flowers to be grown in this sub-arctic climate. Where conditions permit, the Icelanders have been able to tap steam to power geothermal power stations. Operating such equipment in such an unstable environment has not been without its problems, especially when earthquakes and changing land levels snap the pipes that are buried deep into the ground. There are three geothermal plants at present, at Krafla (by Mývatn), at Svartsengi (near Grindavík, to the southwest of

Reykjavík) and at Nesjavellir, to the south of the lake Thingvallavatn. Svartsengi is the site of one of Iceland's newer attractions, the warm swimming pool known as the 'Blue Lagoon'.

The ice-caps and their glaciers

The main ice-caps dominate the interior of the country, but there are other ice-caps that are important features in more peripheral parts of the island, such as Snæfellsjökull (on Snæfellsnes peninsula), Drangajökull (in the Northwest Fiords) and the neighbouring ice-caps of Mýrdalsjökull and Eyjafjallajökull near the south coast.

Warm and damp winds from the southwest cool when they meet Iceland's mountains, and snow falls on the high ground, building up huge thicknesses of ice. The weight of ice forces it to flow downhill as frozen 'rivers' and these valley glaciers rip up valley walls and turn V-shaped valleys into U-shaped ones. As the mountainsides are ground down by the action of these glaciers, the broken-up rock is pulverised into gravel, sand and dust. Much of this gets caught in the ice itself, turning the ice quite black. As the ice melts, the glacial rivers, heavily laden with suspended matter, carry this ground-down rock towards the coast. All round the coast, but especially in the south, huge areas of sand and gravel (called the 'sandur') have been built up and these form a wide gravelly plain many kilometres wide between the mountains and

Icebergs on Lake Jökulsárlón, at the tip of the glacier called Breidamerkurjökull

the sea. These glacial rivers are extremely powerful and are forever changing their courses, forming a network of braided streams across the flat sandur. It is the power and unpredictability of these rivers that has made travel so difficult in many parts of the country. The most convenient place to see the glaciers is at Skaftafell National Park which is on the south coast. Here, you can easily walk to the snout of the valley glacier Skaftafellsjökull and watch its sediment-laden glacial river gushing out. Many other valley glaciers can be seen from the ring road as it heads eastwards from Skaftafell; the most spectacular sight is the glacial lagoon of Jökulsárlón which has beautiful icebergs floating in it.

Rivers and waterfalls

Iceland's greatest river is the Thjórsá, which flows from Hofsjökull. Like many rivers it has a number of waterfalls on it, though these are relatively small. However, to its west lies the Hvitá, which comes down from Langjökull and has one of the country's finest waterfalls (Gullfoss) on it. In the northeast of the country, the Jökulsá á Fjöllum flows northwards from Vatnajökull and boasts a number of fine waterfalls, including the mighty Dettifoss. As befits a country with a rather damp climate, there are hundreds of notable waterfalls, some of them quite unusual such as Ófærufoss with its natural arch, and Hraunfossar whose water flows *out* of the rock.

The Icelanders certainly do not let all this water go to waste and a number of massive hydro-electric projects have harnessed big rivers (including the Thjórsá) in order to generate electricity. The utilisation of this valuable natural resource has allowed the construction of a large aluminium smelter at Straumsvík (to the west of Reykjavík) which makes uses of this 'clean' form of energy. Indeed, visitors will find Iceland a very clean country, with no smog or pollution dirtying the atmosphere. The country has no workable fossil fuels of its own and the development of geothermal and hydro-electric projects has meant that there are few factory chimneys and few homes with a fireplace.

At Hjálparfoss waterfall the River Fossá tumbles between basalt columns

History

The settlement of Iceland

Since Iceland is situated far out in the northern reaches of the Atlantic and well away from the populated landmasses, it is hardly surprising that it was one of the last parts of Europe to be settled.

Roman coins of around AD300 have been found in southern Iceland but it is unlikely that the Romans themselves ever set foot on the island -the coins were probably brought by later sailors. The first people to actually stay in the country were Irish hermits who started to arrive towards the end of the 8th century. These priests eventually died or left when the Vikings arrived a century later and there are few reminders of their sojourn, but placenames like Papafjördur (near Höfn on the southeastern coast) signify localities where they lived.

At the end of the 8th century there was a great wave of exploration (and plunder!) by Viking seafarers from the Nordic countries of Norway, Sweden and Denmark. In AD793 they sacked Lindisfarne, off the east coast of England, and established colonies in many parts of England, Scotland, Ireland, France and the Faeroes. Once the Vikings had reached the Faeroes, it was not too long before they discovered Iceland, whether by accident or design. In AD860, the Norwegian Naddod landed in the Eastern Fiords (by accident) and in 864 the Swede Gardar Svafarsson sailed round Iceland, demonstrating that it was indeed an island. A little later, Flóki Vilgerdarson spent two years in the country and gave it the name 'Iceland' when he saw ice in the fiord of Vatnsfjördur in the Northwest Fiords. The first people considered as settlers were led by Ingólfur Arnarson and Hjörleifur Hródmarsson, who sailed to Iceland in the AD870s. Their ships moved along the south coast of the country in stages with Ingólfur looking for the high-seat pillars that he had tossed overboard when he sighted land. (In Norwegian long-houses, the roof was supported by pillars, the two main ones on either side of the high-seat and carved with mythical beasts.) He sent his servants in search of them, believing that his gods would bring them ashore at the place he should settle.

The pillars came ashore at a bay Ingólfur named 'Reykjavík' ('Smoky Bay') because of the plumes of warm vapour rising from the district's hot springs.

The date of the start of the Settlement is normally taken as AD874. Groups of new colonists soon started to arrive and the arable land was 'fully' settled around the year AD930. The years 874–930 are really quite remarkable, as this period of colonisation was recorded in writing. The main documents, *The Book of Icelanders* and *The Book of Settlements* describe in great detail the names of the principal settlers, their land and much else about them and their followers. Many of these people came from Norway and they were often led by the scions of landed families who had left their homeland in order to conquer new land or because of the unsettled times in their own country. Many of these men brought slaves (often Irish or Scots) with them but these were later freed. The main areas of population were very similar to those of today – generally in the southwest of the country and along the coastal fringes at places where boats could be brought ashore. Farming was the main occupation with fishing, as yet, of far less importance.

The age of the sagas

In the various communities local parliaments or *Things* were established and these were united in the national *Althing* that was convened at Thingvellir ('The Plain of all Men') on the northern shore of lake Thingvallavatn. The Althing was convened there for the first time in AD930 and the period from then until 1030 is known as the Age of the Sagas. The laws for this body were proposed by Úlfljót, a wise man who had been sent to western Norway to study the form of government there. The Althing was given legislative and judicial power and convened once a year. It was presided over by the Lawspeaker, who had to recite one-third of the laws from memory each year during his three-year period of office. Neither he nor the Althing had any executive power, something that eventually led to the chaotic collapse of the country due to the almost incessant warring between individual chieftains (the *godi*) and their families.

The Saga Age, with its feuding and politicking, was full of noteworthy events (many of them rather bloody) which were later recorded in the Sagas, a number of which have survived to

Church and farmhouse at Thingvellir. This is where the Althing used to assemble, and it is here that the declaration of the Icelandic republic was made in 1944

this day. The Viking traditions of honour, loyalty to one's family and the duty of taking revenge for slights against the family resulted in blood-letting on a regular basis. The Icelanders often led the Nordic world in literature, and in the 12th and 13th centuries the tales that had previously been passed down orally through the generations were recorded on paper, no doubt adding a few embellishments on the way! The Sagas are immensely important documents as they deal not only with social and political events in Iceland, but also describe the daily lives of the people, their values, their fears and their dealings with other countries. In this last respect, they also preserve details of events and customs in Norway, Scotland and other countries visited by Icelanders.

The colonies in Greenland and America

The Icelanders maintained the seafaring traditions they had brought from their original homelands, and were not unused to sailing across unknown waters. Greenland is only 180 miles (290km) from Iceland and the first Icelander known to have reached Greenland was Gunnbjörn Úlfsson. This icy land's first actual settler, however, was Eiríkur Thorvaldsson, better-known as Eirík the Red, who spent a three-year exile (imposed for a killing) exploring southern Greenland around AD982. He returned to Iceland briefly to persuade others to join him in setting up a colony and used the rather exotic name 'Greenland' to help him attract potential settlers. Colonies were set up on the west coast and were known to exist up to at least the 15th century, but for some as yet unknown reason the people either all died or left. Some remains of a settlement exist at a place known to Icelanders as Brattahlíd (or Qassiarsuk to the Greenlanders) and many visitors to Iceland visit this historic place on a day trip to Narssarssuaq from Reykjavík.

From Greenland, it was not much farther to North America, and although today's history books usually credit Christopher Columbus with 'discovering' America, Icelanders were the first Europeans to land on North American soil – 500 years before Columbus. The best-known

*Leif Eiríksson –
Iceland's greatest
navigator*

explorer was Eirík the Red's son, Leif Eiríksson,
who visited a place he called Vinland
('Wineland') on account of the grapes he found
growing there. This may have been southern
Labrador or farther south. Colonies were set up
over a period of time but they became involved
in fighting with the native Indians and never
prospered. The tales of these daring
adventures are preserved for prosperity in the
Vinland Sagas.

The centuries of foreign domination

As many of Iceland's original settlers came from
Norway, the Norwegian throne had long held
the view that Iceland should come under
Norwegian control. Religion was used as a
political tool in this task and the king, Ólaf
Tryggvason, sent missionaries to Iceland in
order to convert the people to Christianity.
Violence was not an unusual means of

'persuading' some people of the correctness of these new ideas. Many people did adopt Christianity, including many chieftains, but pagan deities were still held in high regard. Almost inevitably, religion became a divisive issue in the Althing, and at its meeting in AD1000, a pragmatic decision was taken that the people should take up the new religion – but still be allowed to worship pagan gods in private. The Lawspeaker at this momentous event was Thorgeir, a wise man who had been entrusted with resolving a conflict that was leading to civil war.

The church now began to establish itself as a real force in the country, and since many of the churchmen came from Norway, this increased the Norwegian king's influence over Iceland. Bishoprics were established at Skálholt in the southwest and Hólar in the north, and in time these became important centres of learning. The bishops' power increased tremendously when tithes (taxes of one-tenth of income) were introduced in AD1097, bringing the role of the church into the centre stage of politics.

By the 13th century, a few dominant families held sway in the country. Alliances and allegiances frequently changed and the Norwegian king was often involved in the chieftains' intrigues. The most famous man of this time was Snorri Sturluson (1179-1241). He served twice as Lawspeaker and was constantly embroiled in political machinations. Aside from his warring escapades, he was also one of the country's greatest writers and is credited with writing *The Younger Edda*, *Heimskringla* and possibly some Sagas too. The king used Snorri to help him increase his hold over the people, but it was not until 1262, when continual feuding was leading the country to collapse, that the chieftains called upon King Hákon to intervene and stop the slide into anarchy.

Iceland remained under foreign rule from 1262 until the middle of the 20th century. Some periods of her history were dark indeed. Norway increased its domination of the country and allowed the church even more power in secular matters as well as religious ones. In 1387, the Kalmar Act of Union joined together

Norway, Sweden and Denmark, but this change had little effect in Iceland. (This piece of power politics later led to Iceland becoming part of Denmark.) Foreign control, nepotism in high places, disease and volcanic eruptions – all of these heaped miseries on the people in the 13th and 14th centuries and daily life became a mere struggle for survival.

Iceland was, however, affected by the Reformation and the 16th century saw more social upheaval. In 1550, Bishop Jón Arason was beheaded at Skálholt and the king seized much of the church's possessions, greatly increasing his own wealth and power. Iceland was regarded as a milch cow, and a poverty-stricken one at that: the king even leased the country's trade to Danish merchants, thus establishing a crippling monopoly that lasted until 1787.

The Icelanders became trapped by this monopoly. It meant they were supplied with putrid goods and had no other supplier to turn to. Petitions to the king were ignored and the

Reykjavík's Lutheran cathedral

BACKGROUND

Austurvöllur, the square in the centre of Reykjavík

country's fortunes plummeted. Matters could hardly have become worse when, in 1662, the king abrogated the original treaty of 1262 and declared himself an absolute monarch.

Although the country remained very poor, the traditions of learning and scholarship stayed alive. The Reformation gave an impetus to the use of the printing press and as well as religious books, secular books were written and more people learned to read and write. There was also an awakening of interest in the Sagas and the Icelander Árni Magnússon (1663–1730), who was a professor of history at the University of Copenhagen, collected great numbers of these ancient writings and transported them to Copenhagen. Unfortunately, a huge fire in 1728 destroyed many of these priceless documents but those that were saved have been carefully protected ever since.

In 1752 two Icelanders, Eggert Ólafsson and Bjarni Pálsson, were sent from Copenhagen to Iceland to survey the country and to report on their findings. Their writings stand as a fascinating account of 18th-century Iceland. Further reports on the state of the country were commissioned and as a result significant changes were made. A postal system was introduced and small-scale industry established. The person most involved in the setting up of these workshops, especially in the Reykjavík area, was the far-sighted bailiff Skúli

Magnússon (1711–1794), who had to fend off the machinations of the powerful Danish merchants in his attempts to improve the lot of his own people. This important foothold in industry led to Reykjavík being granted its municipal charter in 1786, at which time it had a population of only 167!

While these developments promised a much better future, the advances came to an abrupt halt in 1783 when the volcano Laki erupted. This eruption created the biggest lavafield produced by a single eruption in historical times. Poisonous gases filled the air and killed the grass, resulting in starvation for animals and people alike; about 10,000 people lost their lives.

The country's population fell to below 40,000 and drastic measures were needed to help the Icelanders. Reykjavík was now developing as an important centre, so the sees of Skálholt and Hólar were abolished and combined into one which was based in Reykjavík. A new school was established there, and in 1798 the Althing was held for the last time at Thingvellir and then moved to Reykjavík (although it was closed down in 1800).

Skúli Magnússon, an 18th-century entrepreneur who brought something like free trade to Iceland

BACKGROUND

In the 19th century, Iceland found itself dragged into the Napoleonic Wars and the momentous social and political changes that were taking place in mainland Europe. One result of the revolutionary wave that swept through Europe was that the Danish king renounced absolutism and promised important political and social reforms. There was a new awakening of the Icelandic spirit and many Icelanders struggled to win more control over their own lives. One such man, the great patriot Jón Sigurðsson (1811-1879), published his ideas and led the struggle that resulted in the re-establishment of the Althing in 1845. The fight for independence was now well under way.

The fight for independence

A constitutional convention failed to answer the grievances of the people but in 1874, at the celebration to mark the Millennium of the Settlement, King Christian IX of Denmark presented the country with a new constitution. This brought about a new Althing with 36 members, only six of which were to be appointed by the king. Parliament now had enough financial and legislative power to begin the process of building the infrastructure needed by a fledgling nation. Education, transport, banking and fishing were encouraged to develop, but even with all these innovations, the lot of the people was not greatly improved, and between 1870 and 1914 many Icelanders emigrated to North America in search of a new life.

A new constitution was drawn up in 1904 and at last the Icelanders had their own government. Great changes came about as transport and roads were improved, allowing cars to be introduced in the century's second decade. Fishing was by now the country's most important industry and the growing fleet of steam trawlers encouraged even greater development and prosperity.

World War I disrupted trade in many ways but, through necessity, this encouraged the Icelanders to act rather more independently of Denmark in economic affairs. In 1918, a 25-year agreement was made whereby the Icelanders

Ship in the museum
at Akranes

gained greater control over their internal affairs while Denmark maintained responsibility for external affairs such as defence and foreign policy.

The celebrations to mark the Millennium of the Althing in 1930 were a great event, but serious problems – the Depression and World War II – loomed on the horizon. During the war Iceland's strategic position in the middle of the North Atlantic meant that it was a focus of attention for both sides in the conflict. In April 1940 Germany attacked Denmark, thus severing Iceland's links with its capital. One month later, British forces occupied Iceland to prevent Germany from doing the same thing, and in 1941 the United States took over from them. By this time, the Althing had declared that its Union with Denmark had become void because of the German occupation. In these circumstances, the country was declared fully independent at Thingvellir on 17 June 1944, the birthday of Jón Sigurðsson – a most suitable place and date for such an important event.

The Economy

World War II paradoxically brought about a great economic boom in Iceland; roads, bridges and airfields were built, there was more money around and so houses and living conditions became better and people saw their quality of life improving dramatically.

About 40 per cent of the population now live in or near Reykjavík and the rest of the country is essentially a land of small settlements, many of them with a population of less than 1,000-2,000 people; there are only a few 'towns' with a population of over 5,000 or so people. The settlements around the coast are based on fishing, while those of the southwest and parts of the north are predominantly agricultural.

Fishing is of vital importance to the economy and to the well being of the people since it accounts for over 70 per cent of the country's exports. That is why unarmed Icelanders were so willing to fight the so-called 'Cod Wars' against Britain in the 1970s. These were disputes over fishing grounds. The country's main fishing ports are Reykjavík and Heimaey (on the Westman Islands). The larger fishing settlements have fish processing plants and these provide work for many, though they suffer when boats take their catches direct to foreign fish markets such as Grimsby in England. In recent years concern about over-fishing has meant that boats have had to limit their catches in order to allow the fish stocks to recover.

The main agricultural activity is sheep farming; there are about 600,000 sheep on the island. Many of them are driven to the highlands for summer grazing as this allows the farmers to keep the best land for growing hay, the principal crop, which is used as winter feed for sheep, horses and cattle. When the original settlers arrived, about one-third of the land was covered by woodland. However, tree-cutting for establishing settlements, for building materials and for producing charcoal has destroyed much of the tree cover. When the trees are felled, strong winds rip up the smaller plants and erode the soil, and now much of the land (especially in the highlands) is quite devoid of plant life. Sheep farming has greatly exacerbated this problem and it is now a major

New times bring new ways. Fish farms such as those at Hraunsfjördtur make a substantial contribution to Iceland's economy

environmental issue. Parts of the highlands have been fenced off and a long-term programme of reseeding the deserts is underway. Farmers are thus under pressure to reduce their flocks and diversify the use of their land and a number of them look towards tourism as a means of maintaining their standard of living, hence the growth of farmhouse accommodation for summer visitors. The standard of living is so high because the worldwide increase in fish consumption since World War II has greatly benefited the Icelanders. Full employment has been an important goal in economic life and this is considered to be more important than the problem of inflation, which was extremely high in the 1980s and was a real threat to economic growth.

In general, the Icelanders are attempting to diversify their economy and rely less on fishing. Hydro-electric power stations produce enough energy for huge plants like the aluminium smelter at Straumsvík and other energy-intensive projects are always being discussed. The engineering industry's expertise in such areas as well-drilling and making equipment for the fishing industry is now being used to

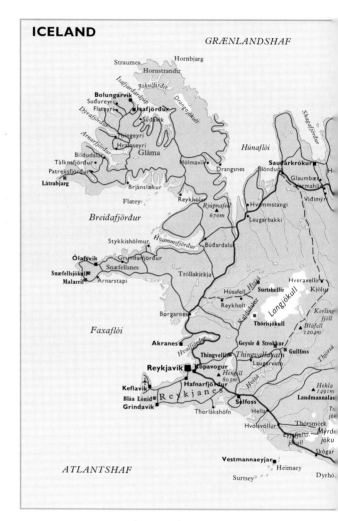

increase the export trade.
The emergence of Iceland onto the world sta
has given Icelanders much to debate and the
political life of the country reflects their hopes
and their fears. The elected Althing meets in
Reykjavík and governments since
Independence in 1944 have often been

coalitions, some of them rather short-lived. The presidency is not directly linked to politics since presidential elections and general elections are quite separate and some presidents have been non-party figures who have gained national positions in non-political roles.

WHAT TO SEE

Planning an Itinerary

Iceland is a unique country and it makes special demands on its visitors. Once you have decided Iceland is the place for you, this book helps to answer the next questions: How do I get there? Which places should I visit? What can I expect to find? None of these questions can be answered in isolation. Hard and inescapable facts like the amount of time and money you have available, the number of people in your group, and whether or not someone is willing to drive in often difficult conditions, narrow your options down at the start. In addition, visitors with a special interest such as geology or ornithology will undoubtedly have specific places in mind before they arrive.

First-time visitors are recommended to consider taking a vehicle round the ring road which encircles Iceland, and also visiting some places in the southwest and northeast. From Reykjavík, one possible route is:

1 Reykjavík – Thingvallavatn – Strokkur – Gullfoss – Selfoss (2/3 days)
2 Selfoss – Vík – Skaftafell – Egilsstadir (4/5 days)
3 Egilsstadir – Mývatn – Jökulsárgljúfur National Park – Húsavík – Akureyri (3/4 days)
4 Akureyri – Borgarnes – Reykjavík (2/3 days)

These four sections give a total of 11/15 days – but even 15 days is rushing it; three weeks in total is really recommended, including a day in Reykjavík and at least one day spare for unforeseen delays.

However, with careful planning, it is quite feasible to see many of the places in this suggested itinerary in a two-week holiday. The 'What to See' section of this book gives background information on all the most important places met on this itinerary – and much more. Visitors not using a car have less flexibility in their arrangements but may wish to consider the route mentioned above, using public transport. However, instead of the journeys off the ring road, they might like to go on the one-day 'Golden Circle' tour from Reykjavík (to Thingvallavatn, Strokkur and Gullfoss) and the one-day 'Northern Highlights' tour from Mývatn to the Jökulsárgljúfur National Park. Visitors without a car have the freedom to stay a little longer in certain areas, knowing that it *should* be possible to return to Reykjavík or Egilsstadir (for connections for planes and ferries) in one day. It should be remembered that scheduled buses cross the interior (by the Kjölur and Sprengisandur routes) and these services can be used to save time as well as giving an opportunity to see the interior. Visitors generally find the Akureyri – Reykjavík part of the ring road less interesting than other sections and one possible alternative to this journey is to go from Akureyri to Reykjavík across either Kjölur or Sprengisandur.

The 'What to See' section gives a one-to-three star rating to all the places that appear under the individual headings. Reykjavík's sights have been given their own one-to-three star rating to help you plan a day's sightseeing in the capital. Before deciding where to go, read the 'What to See' section and study the tour operators' brochures. These often have maps showing you the routes that tour buses take and might help you choose a suitable route.

As most visitors will be spending some time in Reykjavík and on the ring road (and quite possibly going round all or most of it), the 'What to See' section has been arranged with Reykjavík and the Reykjanes peninsula first, followed by the ring road (the southwest, the south, the Eastern Fiords, the northeast, the north and the west) and lastly, the Northwest Fiords and the interior.

Reykjavík is a clean and green city

REYKJAVÍK

Reykjavík is fascinating. It is also quite unlike the rest of the country, and is full of surprises and contradictions. This is the world's most northerly capital and in many ways it has the features of a 'frontier' town. Huge four-wheel drive vehicles rumble into the city to pick up the family shopping; spare fuel cans, spades and a tow-rope are hung on the vehicles like Christmas decorations. In comparison to that, what other city of only 97,000 could boast a university, over a dozen museums and libraries, numerous galleries, an opera theatre and much much more? Since World War II, when a building boom was started by the occupying forces, the capital has grown and today the city and its suburbs account for some 40 per cent of the country's entire population. This can hardly be good for the long-term development of the country, but this proportion keeps increasing year by year.

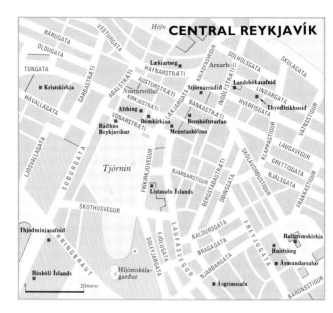

The city is bright and colourful and does not suffer from the pollution so common in other capitals; clean, geothermal energy is used for heating buildings.

The city centre is quite compact so it is possible to see many of the places mentioned below without your feet aching too much. The oldest part is around **Austurvöllur** and there are many interesting buildings in this district. This is also one of the traditional shopping areas, as is Bankastræti and its continuation Laugavegur. The opening of the Kringlan shopping mall (to the east of the city centre) has taken many customers away from 'downtown Reykjavik', so the shops in the city centre have had their winter environment made rather

safer and more pleasant by having geothermal under-pavement heating installed to thaw the winter snow and ice. Many of the city's older houses have a corrugated iron exterior but there is nothing temporary about these structures. In various parts of the city, some of the smaller examples of these old buildings have been (literally) uprooted and re-positioned on top of new foundations – a high-tech solution to the problem of how to maintain links with the past. The most important building material is concrete as concrete structures can be erected quickly, an important factor when bad weather can play havoc with building schedules. Although some of the buildings, notably tall apartment blocks, are similar to the bland structures found in almost any European city, there are numerous interesting designs that indicate how something as 'mundane' as concrete can be used to good effect.

Perhaps surprising for a city so far north, there are many trees, especially in the gardens of the older houses. Many open spaces have statues in them and a number of sculptors' collections are displayed in small gardens. The harbour area is well worth exploring – you can watch the fishing boats unload at the northernmost part of the harbour; worth a walk. **Tjörnin** is very pleasant and should be visited. **Hallgrímskirkja** and **Öskjuhlíð** are both excellent viewpoints.

Bus services are frequent and the two most convenient stations are at **Lækjartorg** square and at **Hlemmur**; taxis are also numerous and reasonably priced. Up-to-date details on what to see in Reykjavík, together with the latest information on opening times can be obtained from the free publications *Around Iceland* and *What's on in Reykjavík*.

Although most visitors go to Iceland to enjoy the outdoor life, it is worth spending some time in Reykjavík in order to explore some of the places listed below. Visitors who are in Reykjavík in June or July will have many hours of daylight and it would be quite possible to see many of these in one day. Remember to get a map from the **Tourist Information Centre** (at Bankastræti 2).

◆
AÐAALSTRÆTI 10
Originally built as a shed in 1752, this is Reykjavík's oldest building. It is now a restaurant.

◆◆◆
ALTHINGISHÚSIÐ (PARLIAMENT HOUSE)
This sombre-looking building in Austurvöllur was built in 1881, before Iceland's independence from Denmark, hence the carving of the Danish crown on the façade. Other carvings on the front wall depict a dragon, a vulture, a giant and a bull – spirits that would have been important to Ingólfur Arnarson, one of the first settlers in this strange land.

◆◆◆
ÁRBÆR
Árbær is situated at the eastern end of the city, near the salmon river Ellidaár. It is a marvellous collection of old buildings which have been assembled from many parts of the country. A turf-roofed church is one of the highlights here.
Summer opening: Tuesday to Sunday 10.00-18.00hrs.
Closed: Monday.

◆
ÁRNAGARÐUR (MANUSCRIPT INSTITUTE)
This building in Sudurgata was named after Árni Magnússon, a man who did much to discover and take ancient Icelandic manuscripts and take them to Copenhagen, then Iceland's capital, for safe-keeping. Now that Iceland has the facilities to deal with the preservation of these invaluable documents, they have been

REYKJAVÍK ENVIRONS

returned for study and display in their rightful home.
Summer opening: Tuesday, Thursday and Saturday 14.00–16.00hrs. *Closed:* Sunday, Monday, Wednesday and Friday.

◆◆ ARNARHÓLL (EAGLE'S MOUND)

Overlooking the eastern side of the harbour, this prominent hillock is topped by a statue of Ingólfur Arnarson, the city's first settler. He is depicted on his ship, looking out at the smoking hot springs of his intended

landing place, Reykjavík.

◆ ÁSGRÍMSSAFN (ÁSGRÍMUR JÓNSSON MUSEUM)

Situated at Bergstaðarstræti 74, this was the home of the sculptor Asgrímur Jónsson (1876-1958). It contains examples of his work.
Summer opening: Tuesday to Sunday 13.00-16.00hrs. *Closed:* Mondays. *Winter opening:* Sunday, Tuesday, Thursday, Saturday 13.30-16.00hrs. *Closed:* Monday, Wednesday, Friday.

set in a little park with many of the sculptor's works on display. He lived from 1893-1982.
Summer opening: daily 10.00-16.00hrs. *Winter opening:* daily 13.00-16.00hrs. The park is always open.

◆◆◆ AUSTURVÖLLUR

By happy coincidence, this pleasant square in the centre of the old city was the original 'homefield' of the country's first settler, Ingólfur Arnarson. In its centre stands a statue of Jón Sigurdsson (1811-1879), the national leader who did so much to raise the political conciousness and national aspirations of the Icelandic people. The Althingishúsið (Parliament House) stands to the south of the square and Dómkirkjan (the Cathedral) stands to its southeast.
Just to the west of the square, Kirkjustræti leads past a little park in which there is a statue of Skúli Magnússon, a bailiff who encouraged the development of industry in Reykjavík in the 18th century.

◆ ÁSMUNDUR SVEINSSON'S HOUSE

Ásmundur Sveinsson is one of Iceland's most famous sculptors. His house, which is at Freyjugata 41, is open to the public.
Open: Monday to Friday 16.00-22.00hrs, Saturdays and Sundays 14.00-22.00hrs.

◆◆ ÁSMUNDUR SVEINSSON'S STUDIO

This remarkable spherical concrete building in Sigtún is

◆◆◆ BERNHÖFTSTORFAN (BERNHOFT'S GROUP)

This pleasing group of old wooden buildings at the western end of Bankastræti would have been lost to 'redevelopment' had it not been for a great effort to save them. The Tourist Information Centre is in the centre of this charming little enclave.
A large open-air chess board is set out in front of the buildings. Keep a sharp look-out for future Grandmasters here.

WHAT TO SEE

◆
DÓMKIRKJAN (LUTHERAN CATHEDRAL)

Despite its rather plain looks, this corrugated-iron building is the country's main church. It is in Austurvöllur.
Open: Monday to Friday 09.00-17.00hrs.

◆
GRASAGARÐUR (BOTANIC GARDENS)

A cross-section of Iceland's plants is gathered in this little park. Look for it near Holtavegur, southeast of the large white exhibition hall.

◆◆◆
HALLGRÍMSKIRKJA (HALLGRÍMUR'S CHURCH)

Tall and beautiful, this church dominates the city's skyline from the top of Skólavördustígur. Its height is emphasised by the slender concrete pillars representing basalt columns, which are common features in some districts of the country.

Hallgrímskirkja's modern gothic

The church's observation platform (which is reached by a lift) gives wonderful views of the city and is certainly worth visiting.
Open: Tuesday to Sunday 10.00-18.00hrs. *Closed:* Monday.
In front of the church is a statue of Leif Eiríksson, founder of an Icelandic colony in North America. This bold statue was a gift from the people of the United States to celebrate the Althing's Millenium anniversary in 1930.

◆
HÁSKÓLI ÍSLANDS (UNIVERSITY OF ICELAND)

The university area is by Sudurgata. The main building was built in 1940. Before then, students had to go abroad to further their education. In front of it is a statue of the 11th century scholar, Sæmundur the Learned, riding on the back of a seal. The legend is that Sæmundur was returning from Paris to Iceland when the Devil (disguised as a seal) offered him a lift in return for his soul. Sæmundur is depicted hitting the seal over the head with a book just before dry land is reached!
The University's art collection is at Oddi in Sudurgata.
Summer opening: daily 13.30-18.00hrs. Admission free.

◆
HNITBJÖRG

Sculptor Einar Jónsson (1874-1954) lived in this stark concrete building, which now contains a collection of his work. It is in Njardargata.
Summer opening: Tuesday to Sunday 13.30-16.00hrs. *Closed:*

Monday. *Winter opening:*
Saturday and Sunday
13.30-16.00. *Closed:* Monday to
Friday. The museum is closed in
December and January but the
garden is open all year round.

◆ HÖFÐI

Höfði, the Municipal Reception
House, is just off Borgartún. This
is the building that won a place
in history as the venue for the
Gorbachev–Reagan summit in
1986.

◆◆ KJARVALSSTAÐIR (MUNICIPAL ART GALLERY)

Kjarvalsstadir stands in the park
known as Miklatún, on the
northern side of Miklabraut.
This gallery is named after the
Icelandic artist Jóhannes Kjarval
(1885-1972) and there are a
number of his works on show.
Open: daily during exhibitions
11.00-18.00hrs.

◆ KRINGLAN

Reykjavík's first indoor shopping
mall is in the district of Kringlan,
which is to the east of the city
centre. It has lots of shops and a
very large supermarket; the
latter is particularly useful for
visitors and the prices are quite
reasonable – by Icelandic
standards.

◆ KRISTSKIRKJA (ROMAN CATHOLIC CATHEDRAL)

Concrete has been used to
create a neo-gothic structure
here, a combination of material
and styles that comes as
something of a shock. It was
built in 1929.
Open: at all times.

Höfði – where East met West

◆ LANDSBÓKASAFNIÐ (NATIONAL LIBRARY)

Built in 1908, this is Iceland's
principal library, and also
houses the country's archives.
Open: Monday to Friday
09.00-19.00hrs, Saturday
10.00-12.00hrs.
Closed: Sunday, and also
Saturdays from June to August.

◆◆◆ LAUGARDALUR

This is the site of the city's main
outdoor swimming pool – a
wonderful place, but it can get
busy. The city's campsite and
the newer of the two youth
hostels are just to the east of the
pool.
Open: Monday to Friday
07.00-20.30hrs, Saturday
07.30-17.30hrs, Sunday
08.00-17.30hrs.

WHAT TO SEE

Landsbókasafnid's elegant façade

◆◆
LISTASAFN ÍSLANDS (NATIONAL GALLERY OF ICELAND)

This tall and attractive building was once used as an ice house, where the ice taken off Tjörnin was stored before being used to freeze fish. Today, it holds the country's main collection of paintings and other art forms, as well as being a venue for touring exhibitions. It is at Fríkirkjuvegur 7.
Open: Tuesday to Sunday 12.00-18.00hrs. *Closed*: Monday. Admission free.

◆
MENNTASKÓLINN (HIGH SCHOOL)

Situated in Lækjargata this prominent building was built in 1846 and housed the Althing until the Althingihúsid was built.

◆◆
NÁTTÚRUGRIPASAFNID (NATURAL HISTORY MUSEUM)

A large collection of rocks and minerals as well as examples of plants and animals indigenous to Iceland is housed here. The location is Hverfisgata 116.
Open: Sunday, Tuesday, Thursday and Saturday 13.00-16.00hrs. *Closed*: Monday, Wednesday and Friday. Admission free.

◆
NORRÆNA HÚSID (NORDIC CENTRE)

Built opposite the University, the centre's function is to hold exhibitions on subjects dealing with the Nordic countries.
Open: daily during exhibitions 14.00-19.00hrs.

◆◆◆
ÖSKJUHLÍD (ASH TREE HILL)

This prominent hill near the Hotel Loftleidir has the city's hot water storage tanks on its summit. These are topped by the city's newest landmark – a revolving restaurant.
The hill gives excellent views and is definitely worth ascending, even if you aren't staying at the hotel.

◆
SIGURDUR ÓLAFSSON MUSEUM

Situated at Laugarnestangi 70, this museum shows works by the sculptor Sigurdur Ólafsson, who lived from 1908 to 1982. *Open*: Monday, Wednesday and Thursday 20.00-22.00hrs and Saturday, Sunday 14.00-18.00hrs. *Closed*: Tuesday and Friday.

◆◆
STJÓRNARRÁÐID (GOVERNMENT HOUSE)

Built in Bankastræti in 1756, this was originally used by the Danish government as a prison. It now serves as offices for the country's president. The statues in front are of Christian IX of Denmark and Hannes Hafstein, the first Minister (leader of government).

◆
THJÓDLEIKHUSID (NATIONAL THEATRE)

The exterior of this dark building in Hverfisgata has features representing basalt pillars; these were modelled on the waterfall Svartifoss, which visitors can see at Skaftafell National Park.

◆◆
THJÓDMINJASAFNIÐ (NATIONAL MUSEUM)

Opened in 1950 this museum holds a fascinating collection of historical objects, including examples of furniture and clothing worn in bygone days and equipment from farms and the fishing industry. It is at Sudurgata 41. *Summer opening*: Tuesday to Sunday 11.00-16.00hrs. *Closed*: Monday. *Winter opening*:

Sunday, Tuesday, Thursday, Saturday 11.00-16.00hrs. *Closed*: Monday, Wednesday, Friday. Admission free.

◆◆◆
TJÖRNIN (THE POND)

Every bustling city needs a place of peace and quiet, and this is Reykjavík's. The pond is kept partially ice-free (by warm water) during the winter so it is an all-year haven for birds; the best place for them is at the northeastern corner, nearest Bankastræti. The Rádhús Reykjavíkur (the large and very new City Hall) stands at the northwestern corner. The lakeside walk offers a pleasant stroll and as well as a number of statues to look at, there are information boards showing the types of birds (ducks, swans, geese and arctic terns) that can be seen.

◆
VIDEY

This small island just to the northeast of the city is reached by a ferry from Sundahöfn. Once owned by Ingólfur Arnarson, there was a church on it in the 10th century. The most important building on it today is Videyjarstofa, built by Skúli Magnússon in 1755 and the country's oldest building still in its original form.

Accommodation

Reykjavík has a wide variety of accommodation, ranging from internationally known names like the **Holiday Inn** at Sigtún 38, (tel: (91) 68900) to a couple of youth hostels (Laufásvegur 41, (tel: (91) 24950) and Sundlaugavegur (tel: (91) 38110).

WHAT TO SEE

Icelandair owns two hotels, **Hotel Loftleidir** (tel: (91) 22322) which is to the east of the city's airport and **Hotel Esja** (tel: (91) 82200) at Sudurlandsbraut 2 and visitors on a 'short break' holiday may well be staying at one of these hotels. **Hotel Borg** (Pósthússtræiti 11, (tel: (91) 11440) is an older hotel right in the centre of the city and another well known hotel is **Hotel Holt** (Bergstadastraeti 37, (tel: (91) 25700) which boasts its own art collection. **Hotel Gardur** at Hringbraut (tel: (91) 15656/ 15918) is in the University area; it's student accommodation made available for tourists in the summer.

Tour operators will have full details of all these and other establishments, together with information on the guesthouses and private homes where visitors can stay.

Nightlife

Entertainment is generally not cheap, especially when going out for a meal or a few drinks. Pubs are new to Iceland and can be crowded at weekends. Although they might be reasonably quiet early in the evening, most customers tend to turn up late in the evening and join the end of the queue to get in! Some pubs, like **Gaukur á Stöng** (Tryggvagata 22) and **Fógetinn** (Adalstræti 10), have live music. The large and 'glamorous' places are **Hotel Ísland** (Ármúli 9), **Súlnasalur** (Hotel Saga at Hagatorg) and **Danshöllin** (in Brautarholt) and these may have internationally known artistes and groups appearing as well as Icelandic

artistes. There are numerous discos in the city but it is best to consult the local tourist information to find out which ones might suit your taste in music.

Two shows worth seeing are: **'Light Nights'** at Tjarnargata 10e; this is an English-language show with songs and stories of former days in Iceland.

'The Volcano Show' at Hellusundi 6a; this is a small cinema showing marvellous films of volcanic eruptions and wildlife.

The main sources of information on nightlife in the capital are *What's on in Reykjavík* and *News from Iceland*. The Tourist Information Centre will be able to supply the most up-to-date information.

Restaurants

The capital boasts a range and variety of restaurants. Apart from the hotel restaurants, eating places can be found in or around the city centre and only a short distance from the main places that visitors will want to see. Many, like **Jonathan Livingstone Seagull** (Tryggvagata 6) specialise in fish dishes, while visitors with a taste for game might like to try **Eldvagninn** (Laugavegur 73). Some of the restaurants have traditional decor and one such interesting place is **Lækjarbrekka** (Bankastræti 2) which is in a delightful wooden building near the Tourist Information Centre. **Naust** (Vesturgata 6–8) is most unusual as it is designed as the interior of an old sailing ship. Apart from restaurants serving traditional cuisine, there are places such as **Asía** (Laugavegur 10a) and **Bandidos** (Hverfisgata 56), serving Asian and Mexican food respectively.

At the cheaper end of the range, there are places like the **Hard Rock Café** (in Kringlan), which serves hamburgers, and the **Pizza Hut** (at Sudurlandsbraut 2 and handy for the campsite), predictably selling pasta. It may be useful to remember that there is a caféteria in the BSÍ coach station; this is at Vatnsmýrarvegur.

Visitors can get fuller details of places to eat in the free brochure *What's on in Reykjavík*, an invaluable guide to the city.

Shopping

Reykjavík is a cosmopolitan shopping place, with goods available from all over the world. Gift shops of interest include **The Handknitting Association of Iceland** at Skólavördustígur 19 and **The Icelandic Handcrafts Centre** at the 'Falcon House' (Hafnarstræti 3), where you can enjoy browsing through woollens, jewellery and pottery. Nearby is the Álafoss woollen shop at Vesturgata 2.

The Rammagerdin shops also sell fine woollen wear and they are found in the Hotel Loftleidir, Hotel Esja, in the Kringlan shopping mall and in the city centre at Hafnarstræti 19; the hotel shops are open seven days a week from 08.00-20.00hrs.

Reykjavík's weather does not normally encourage street traders, but some woollen goods may be on sale at stalls at the corner of Lækjartorg and Austurstræti.

Another good place for woollen goods is the Álafoss factory shop, located in the small community of the same name near Mosfellsveit, a suburb just to the northeast of the capital. It sells high quality goods at very competitive prices.

Lækjarbrekka restaurant

WHAT TO SEE

THE REYKJANES PENINSULA

With the Mid-Atlantic Ridge running right along it, this peninsula has a long history of volcanic activity. Most visitors who arrive in Iceland by air will land at **Keflavík**, on the peninsula's northern coast. The 30 miles (48km) journey to Reykjavík will take them past a number of the region's lavafields. Eruptions have occurred since the Settlement – the founding of Iceland – and the area is still prone to earthquakes.

Lava covers much of the land, leaving only a few places where animals can graze. However, the surrounding sea is very rich and there are important fishing ports at settlements (villages) such as Grindavík, Keflavík and Hafnarfjördur. Racks of fish hanging up to dry will be seen along the coast.

◆
BESSASTADIR

This historic site on Reykjanes' northern coast is the official residence of Iceland's president. The present building is over 200 years old. The land on which it stands once belonged to Snorri Sturluson, a colourful historical figure, but the king of Norway confiscated it when he fell out of favour. The little church that stands close to the house was built between 1777 and 1823 and has fine stained glass windows.

◆◆◆
BLUE LAGOON

Just to the north of **Grindavík** lies the outdoor swimming pool known as the 'Blue Lagoon'. Beside the pool are the bright silver-coloured towers and pipes of the **Svartsengi** geothermal power station. Since the hot groundwater used by the power station is rather salty, heat exchangers are employed to warm fresh water for the use of consumers, and the spent brine is allowed to pour out onto the surrounding lavafield. This run-off water is blue in colour because of its suspended solids and is wonderfully warm. It is one of Iceland's most popular tourist attractions and is becoming known worldwide because of the water's benefits to sufferers of skin ailments such as psoriasis.

Summer opening: daily 10.00–22.00hrs. *Winter opening:* Monday to Friday 14.00–21.00hrs, Saturday and Sunday 10.00–21.00hrs.

◆
HAFNARFJÖRDUR

This settlement of about 15,000 people has a busy harbour and has long been an important trading place; English traders were here in the 15th century but were driven out by German merchants.

Sjóminjasafn Íslands, the **Icelandic Maritime Museum**, stands in Vesturgata, suitably close to the harbour. It houses many mementoes of shipping, including models of the rather frail craft that were used to fish the nearby waters.

Summer opening: Tuesday to Sunday 14.00-18.00hrs. *Closed:* Monday. *Winter opening:* Saturday and Sunday 14.00-18.00hrs. *Closed:* Monday. The municipal **folk museum** stands close by. Another notable building in the town is the **Institute of Culture and Fine Art** at Strandgata 34 which stages concerts and exhibitions throughout the year (open daily except Tuesday, 14.00-19.00hrs). Just to the southwest of Hafnarfjördur lies the little bay of **Straumsvík**, the site of a very large aluminium smelter. This consumes a massive amount of electricity and was built to help utilise the country's vast resources of hydro-electric energy.

◆◆
KRÍSUVÍK

The lake of **Kleifarvatn** lies almost in the middle of Reykjanes and at its south-western corner is the volcanically active site of Krísuvík. Sulphur was once mined here, but now it is better known as the most convenient area with mud pools for visitors who are staying in Reykjavík. The coast to the south of Kleifarvatn boasts important bird colonies on the cliffs of **Krísuvíkurberg**, where

Blue Lagoon – heat, health and happiness

kittiwakes, guillemots, razorbills and puffins can be seen. The area around Kleifarvatn is protected and is known as **Reykjanesfólkvangur**; a number of marked paths lead through lavafields and these provide interesting walks. One small island that can be seen from Krísuvíkurberg (and from around Grindavík) is **Eldey**, where the last of the world's great auks was killed in 1844.

Accommodation

Kevlavík is the best-served settlement on Reykjanes for accommodation and **Hotel Keflavík** (tel: (92) 14377) and the **Flughótel** (tel: (92) 15222) are convenient for the international airport. The popular **Blue Lagoon** has its own guesthouse (tel: (92) 68650) for those visitors who want to stay.

Shopping

Hafnarfjördur is a good shopping centre but it does not really cater for the tourist trade as it really is an industrial town. To its west, Keflavík serves much of the peninsula's northwest coast, while on the south coast there are shops in Grindavík and Thorlákshöfn.

SOUTHWESTERN ICELAND

The southwestern corner of Iceland is by far the most populated area of the country, and the portion that lies to the east of Reykjavík is the richest agricultural area. The good farming land supports many herds of cattle, horses and sheep and much of the country's grass is grown here. There are also many places where natural hot water occurs.

This region contains many of the country's most interesting tourist sites and most visitors spend some time here; however, it must be remembered that it is also one of the wetter areas.

◆◆
FLJÓTSDALUR

Fljótsdalur is the little valley that lies just to the west of the Eyjafjallajökull ice-cap and its lush green hillside is in stark contrast to the black sandur that lies to the south. This has been a prosperous farming district for a long time and it was the setting for the wonderful *Njáls Saga*, which took place around the turn of the 11th century. Numerous farms near here belonged to characters in this violent drama and the hero, Gunnar Hámundarson, lived at the farm of **Hlídarendi**. The farm still exists and a lovely little church is perched on the hillside beside the present farmhouse. This offers a wide view over the countryside and towards the ice-caps. The story, which is one of the most powerful of the Sagas, reaches its climax in the burning alive of Gunnar's friend Njál in his farmhouse; this happened at Bergthórshvoll, a farm which lies to the south of the settlement of **Hvolsvöllur**.

◆◆◆
GEYSIR AND STROKKUR

The northern limit of the geothermal energy sources in southwest Iceland is where the

Strokkur's spectacular waterworks

country's most famous waterspout, the Great Geysir, is to be found. It has given its name to all waterspouts (or geysers) as it is (or rather, was) quite spectacular. In the middle of the 18th century Eggert Ólafsson and Bjarni Pálsson visited Geysir during their travels around the island. They described the start of the geyser's eruption as being marked by 'a subterraneous rumbling and gentle detonations'. They estimated the height to which Geysir threw water to be 360 feet (110m)! When the eruption was over they used a plumb-line to determine the depth of the geyser but their Icelandic guide became very concerned, telling them that 'it was not permitted to man to examine such mysterious places, because the powerful spirits who reside in them always punish those who attempt to dive into their secrets'.

Travellers in Victorian times also marvelled at this phenomenon but now, sadly, it lies dormant, and there is only a large pool of hot water which is artificially spouted on special occasions.

However, only a few metres away, Strokkur ('Gusher') attracts tourists by the busload. The water level in its tube rises and falls rhythmically until it suddenly spouts a column of hot water some 65 to 130 feet (20–40m) into the air – soaking all those over-keen photographers who get too close! This spouting occurs every few minutes and is not to be missed.

◆◆◆
GULLFOSS

Iceland is a land of waterfalls and its best known, and arguably the most beautiful, is Gullfoss ('Golden Falls'), so-called because of the rainbow that graces the double falls in sunny weather. This is where the **Hvítá**, a grey-coloured river carrying meltwater and sediment from the Langjökull ice-cap, thunders over the fall, sending huge clouds of spray downwind. The river has carved a fascinating canyon downstream of the waterfall.

◆◆◆
HEKLA

Much of Iceland's farmland has been at the mercy of volcanoes, but the most feared of them is the notorious Hekla. This is the mountain that was once considered to be the entrance to Hell, so great were its destructive powers; it has erupted numerous times since the Settlement, most recently in 1991.

The year 1104 was a momentous one for the farmers who lived in the shadow of Hekla. Its eruptions threw a vast amount of ash over good farming land, and completely destroyed many farms. By using information in the Sagas, archaeologists have been able to locate one of these farms, **Stöng**, and in 1939 it was released from its ash tomb. The farmhouse walls were still standing, as were the remains of the building's internal structure. In 1974 a reconstruction of Stöng was built only a few kilometres to the southwest and named

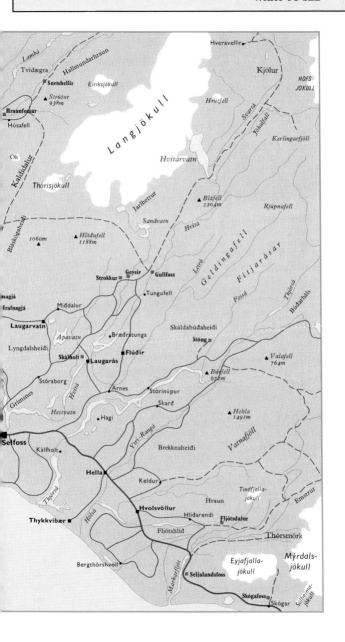

WHAT TO SEE

Thjódveldisbærinn. This is situated by the mountain Búrfell (and very near the mountain's hydro-electric power station) and is rather more accessible than Stöng. This wonderfully interesting building painstakingly recreates Stöng as it would have looked at the moment of its internment. The long hall (with its central fireplace), the women's room, the pantry and the communal toilet are all furnished within substantial walls made of lavablocks and turf.

A journey through Hekla's lavafields and ashfields is a salutary reminder of how people live at the mercy of nature's whims. Hekla can erupt with little or no warning and a big eruption could wipe out much of the country's best farmland; a possibility that could have drastic repercussions for all Icelanders.

To the west of Hekla is Iceland's greatest river, the **Thjórsá**. It flows down from the ice-cap Hofsjökull and has been slowly building up a vast sandur, much of which now forms the rich farmland.

◆◆
HVERAGERÐI

This small settlement on the ring road is Iceland's most successful horticultural centre, boasting numerous glasshouses in which are grown tomatoes, cucumbers, gherkins, flowers – and even a few palm trees. All of this is courtesy of the local supply of natural hot water. Although this can be a peaceful place to wander around during the week, it can be crowded during weekends as the people of Reykjavík come here to buy pot plants or Icelandic-grown cacti. An important health centre has been built just above the settlement and many patients find relief from their ailments by relaxing in hot mud baths.

◆
LAUGARVATN

To the east of Thingvallavatn lies Laugarvatn; the name means 'warm lake' and it is just that – no wonder the windsurfers who come here don't mind too much when they fall in! This is a popular little settlement to visit as it is within easy reach of places such as Thingvallavatn, Strokkur and Gullfoss.

◆
SELFOSS

Southern Iceland's largest town, this important settlement stands on the eastern bank of the Ólfusá. Selfoss is an important centre for the surrounding agricultural area and it has a large dairy on its eastern outskirts. Visitors heading anticlockwise along the ring road should take advantage of shopping facilities in Selfoss as the next important settlement is not met until Höfn, over 240 miles (400km) further on. The settlement's **folk and art museum** (Byggða og Listasafn Arnessyslu) is situated in Tryggvagata.

To the northwest of the settlement lies the mountain **Ingólfsfjall**, named after the country's first settler, Ingólfur Arnarson. Old tales claim that he is buried somewhere near the mountain.

◆◆
SKÁLHOLT

Skálholt was the site of one of Iceland's ancient bishoprics and is one of the country's most historic places. The country's first school was established here and a large wooden church was erected in 1155. However, it is best known for its role in the 16th century Reformation. It was here in 1550 that the Catholic bishop Jón Arason and his sons were beheaded. This barbaric execution took place at a spot now marked by a monument near the present church. Today's church, which was built in the 1950s, is a plain but pleasant building housing a museum in its cellar.

◆◆◆
THINGVALLAVATN, THINGVELLIR AND ALMANNAGJÁ

Thingvallavatn is the country's largest lake and beside it is Thingvellir ('Plain of All Men'), site of the ancient Parliament or Althing. There could hardly be a more spectacular place for a nation to meet, since the northern shore of the lake is formed by a lavafield bounded by two large fissures, Almannagjá to the west and Hrafnagjá to the east. As Iceland is being torn apart by the action of continental drift, these two fissures move farther apart and the fissures are themselves being widened. Indeed, Almannagjá's surface has dropped 4 inches (10cm) in the two decades since 1970. Most of this movement probably took place in 1973 when several earthquakes occurred. Almannagjá is remarkable: the fissure is some 4 miles (7km) long; at places it is wide enough to carry a road and its walls tower above its floor. The gorge's western cliff stands behind the Lögberg ('Law

Thingvallavatn lake

Rock'), a useful sounding board for the Lawspeaker when, in olden days, it was from this spot that he recited the country's laws from memory. To enhance the beauty of the place, the Viking people redirected the river Öxará and allowed it to plunge over the fissure and flow through part of it. The river was put to use, for as well as providing drinking water for the animals, one of its deep pools (Drekkingarhylur) was used for drowning adulteresses and witches. Close to the Lögberg stands a little church whose raised graveyard contains the graves of two poets, Einar Benediksson and Jónas Hallgrímsson.

To the south of the lake stands the mountain **Hengill** and on its northeastern flank is a powerful source of hot water at **Nesjavellir**, which is now being exploited as a source of hot water for the capital.

◆◆
THÓRSMÖRK

Thórsmörk is a small wooded area immediately to the north of the ice-cap **Eyjafjallajökull**. Its spectacular scenery is very popular with Icelanders as well as visitors; this inevitably means that it will be very busy at weekends.

The scenery is quite lush – it has no sheep (which would nibble the greenery) on account of the wild unbridged rivers that run either side of it. The track to Thórsmörk crosses about 20 rivers, four of them extremely dangerous – and that means they can be killers! One of the difficult crossings, through the

Jökulsá, lies just where the river leaves the glacial lagoon of Lónið with small icebergs floating in it. As can be imagined, this route is for four-wheel drive vehicles only and the four big river crossings, especially the Jökulsá, are often busy with visitors from tour buses who are waiting for good photographs of smaller vehicles ploughing through the water. Thórsmörk itself offers many interesting walks to good viewpoints from which the surrounding ice-caps and their valley glaciers can be seen. There are a number of tourist huts and campsites here and the weather is often unusually fine as it is in the rain shadow of Eyjafjallajökull.

◆◆
WESTMAN ISLANDS

The Westman Islands (or Vestmannaeyjar) are a group of small islands just off the southwest coast of the country. Only one of them, **Heimaey**, is inhabited, and its fishing fleet is of vital importance to the Icelandic economy. The harbour and the whole settlement of Heimaey were threatened by a major eruption in 1973 when the volcano **Eldfell** ('Fire Hill') suddenly appeared.

The eruption started without warning one night and the inhabitants were immediately evacuated to the harbour. Fortunately, the fishing fleet was in and a flotilla of boats was able to take the people out to safety at sea. As the volcano spewed out lava and a tall lava wall slowly made its way downhill, a desperate tactic was used in an attempt to save the harbour. Pumps and pipes were brought in (even from abroad) and were used to pour cold sea water over the lava, building up a congealing retaining wall that could force the molten lava to flow away from the settlement and into the sea. This successful struggle against nature lasted weeks and was a truly international effort that managed to save the harbour. Alas, more than 300 homes were lost, some of them buried several metres beneath the new land surface. Many visitors fly to the island on a day trip from Reykjavík. The new volcano, which is still smouldering, can be climbed and the 1973 lava 'extension' to the island lies to the east of Eldfell. Although the eruption caused great devastation, two tangible benefits remain: the lavaflow actually built a seawall which is better than the previous one, and the hot underlying rocks are now utilised to heat water for central heating.

Ten years before, in 1963, the world was intrigued by the sudden 'appearance' of a new volcanic island just a few kilometres southwest of Heimaey. This was **Surtsey**, the tip of a volcano that rose from the seabed some 420 feet (130m) below the Atlantic's waves. The eruption lasted four years, during which time the sea attempted to wash away the ash produced by the eruption and the island's future was only secured when a lavaflow consolidated the more easily eroded banks of ash and cinders. Only scientists are

A bulldozing lavaflow at Heimaey

allowed on the island as it is a valuable natural laboratory for investigating how plants and animals colonise a sterile environment.

The bird cliffs on Heimaey and a number of the other islands have long been the haunt of local people searching for birds' eggs and puffins.

These activities are not for the fainthearted as the cliffs are high and vertical and the winds are often very strong. Few locals go fowling these days and this is now more of a sport than a means of keeping a family fed. Although some of the islands are very small, many support sheep during the summer. You will notice long chains hanging down some of the sheer island cliff faces. These help farmers get the sheep on and off the islands.

WHAT TO SEE

Accommodation

As befits the region's main settlement, Selfoss is well served by hotels – **Hotel Selfoss** (tel: (98) 22500) and **Hotel Thóristún** (tel: (98) 21633). Hveragerđi is a popular place equipped with hotels and a youth hostel. Just beside the ring road is the very impressive **Hotel Örk** (tel: (98) 34700) which specialises in accommodating customers for the local mud baths. Laugarvatn is also a place that attracts many visitors, especially as there are two **Hotel Eddas** – the ML, (tel: (98) 61118) and the HSL (tel: (98) 61154). Hvolsvöllur has **Hotel Hvolsvöllur** (tel: (98) 78187) which is well placed for the morning tour bus to Thórsmörk. The charming wooden **Hotel Valhöll** (tel: (98) 22622) is dramatically set on the northwestern shore of Thingvallavatn. Heimaey's popularity with visitors is matched by the number of hotels and guesthouses and also a youth hostel (tel: (98) 12915); the settlement's main hotels are **Hotel Gestgjafinn** (tel: (98) 12577), **Hotel Thórshamar** (tel: (98) 12900) and **Guesthouse Heimir** (tel: (98) 11515).

Shopping

Selfoss is by far the most important shopping centre in the region, but Hveragerđi, Hella and Hvolsvöllur all have good shops. Farther north shopping facilities are limited, but try Laugarvatn and Flúdir. Heimaey on the Westman Islands offers many types of shops and services.

VATNAJÖKULL AND SOUTHERN ICELAND

Vatnajökull is the world's third-largest ice-cap after Antarctica and Greenland and it dominates the landscape of much of Iceland, especially the southern part. It is basically a huge dome of ice, up to about 3,500 feet (1,000m) thick, which has a few nunataks (ice-free peaks) sticking up through its icy surface. But below this cold exterior lurks a hidden danger – **Grímsvötn**.

Grímsvötn is one of the country's biggest sources of geothermal energy and as it melts the ice it forms a huge lake just to the west of the centre of the ice-cap. Every few years the buoyancy of this water lifts the ice up enough to let a torrent of water pour out, causing a huge flood that ends only when the lake's level has fallen by an almost unbelievable 650 feet (200m). This flood emerges at **Skeiđarárjökull**, just to the west of Skaftafell, causing a massive *jökulhlaup* ('glacier burst'). Skeidarájökull is Europe's biggest valley glacier. During one of these floods huge chunks of ice break off the glacier's snout and these icebergs are carried seawards.

Icelanders have been crossing Vatnajökull for hundreds of years but while that was originally done through necessity, now it is for pleasure. Tracked vehicles or specially-equipped four-wheel drive vehicles often cross it. One of the ice-cap's outlet glaciers, **Skálafellsjökull**, which is to the southeast of the ice-cap, is used for tourist trips in a snowcat – a most memorable experience. Vatnajökull is joined to the smaller ice-cap of Öræfajökull and one of its peaks, **Hvannadalshnúkur** 6,957 feet (2,119m) is the highest mountain in Iceland.

As the ice-caps send their icy tongues down towards the southern coast, these glaciers rip up the mountainsides and deposit huge quantities of sand along the southern coast. The glaciers, the sandur and the glacial rivers have long made this a difficult place to cross. Indeed it was only when the **Skeidará** was bridged in 1974 that the country had a complete ring road.

The two ice-caps of **Mýrdalsjökull** and **Eyjafjallajökull** might seem to be poor relations of the massive Vatnajökull, but beneath the cold surface of Mýrdalsjökull lies a terrifying force. This is the site of **Katla**, a sub-glacial volcano that has erupted some 16 times since the Settlement, often with tragic results. As the volcano erupts, the ice-cap bursts asunder, releasing an enormous flood whose rate of flow is some five times that of

the Amazon! Those visitors who pass here and remember that Katla's next eruption is reckoned to be overdue may not wish to tarry for too long!

◆◆
DYRHÓLAEY

The promontory of Dyrhólaey is the mainland's most southerly point and its 360 feet (110m) high summit (on which there is a lighthouse) offers fine views over the glacial sands and towards the imposing dome of **Mýrdalsjökull**. Dyrhólaey has a well known natural arch through which small boats can pass – but only with great care!

This is a protected site as the birdlife and the interesting wind-eroded rock formations are of great interest.

◆
KIRKJUBÆJARKLAUSTUR

The settlement with the almost unpronounceable name is the only one between Vík and Höfn. Höfn is about 125 miles (200km) to the east, so it has long been of importance as a resting place before travellers cross the dangerous glacial sands.
Irish priests lived in this district

Dyrhólaey's natural arch

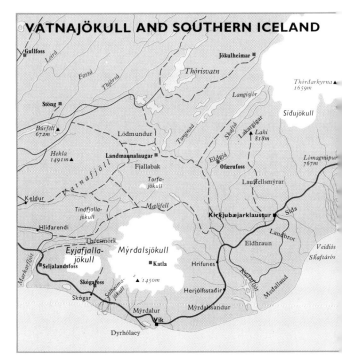

VATNAJÖKULL AND SOUTHERN ICELAND

before the Settlement and a convent was established here in 1186, hence the 'kirk' part of its name. A curious rock formation lies just outside the settlement. This is a level 'floor' of basalt columns which looks very much like the paved floor of an old church, hence its name, **Kirkjugólf**.

◆◆◆
JÖKULSÁRLÓN

A very popular stopping point on the ring road is the glacial lagoon of Jökulsárlón, which lies at the edge of the broad glacier of **Breidamerkurjökull**. This carves icebergs into the lake

and these huge chunks of ice slowly melt and make their way across the lake to the sea. It is an eerie sight and these huge blocks of ice are of various colours – some blue, some white, others quite black with dirt. If you are lucky you might hear or even actually see an iceberg breaking off the glacier. Boat trips on the lake are available in order to get a closer look at these spectacular natural sculptures. This is certainly a place worth stopping at. Another glacial lagoon lies to the southwest of Jökulsárlón; this is **Fjallsárlón** which lies at the foot of the glacier Fjallsjökull.

◆◆
LAKI

Laki is a mountain that lies to the southwest of Vatnajökull and it is situated in the middle of the infamous group of about 100 craters known as Lakagígar. This crater row was formed during the terrible eruptions of 1793 – the most powerful in Iceland in historical times.

The eruptions were preceded by an earthquake that lasted a whole week. Lava began to pour at the beginning of June; the amount of material thrown out is almost beyond the bounds of the imagination: 180,000 cubic feet (5,000 cubic metres) of lava poured out every second. The valley of the Skaftá river was filled with lava to a depth of 650 feet (200m). The activity lasted until February 1784 and by that time the poisonous sulphur dioxide contained in the dust had caused the death of half the country's cattle and three-quarters of its sheep and horses. The calamity was so severe that the possible evacuation of the entire country was discussed. The eruption site can be visited but only in four-wheel drive vehicles as the track to it is extremely rough and the unbridged rivers are unpredictable.

◆◆◆
SKAFTAFELL NATIONAL PARK

At Skaftafell National Park, visitors can see for themselves just how the valley glaciers change the landscape. Skaftafell is an oasis; it is flanked by glaciers and has the huge Skeidarársandur in front of it. But behind the park's campsite is the lush green moorland of Skaftafellsheidi which provides walkers with paths that lead to spectacular views above the Skaftafellsjökull glacier. The moorland also has a charming little waterfall, **Svartifoss**, from whose lip hangs basalt columns. From the campsite, it is only a short walk to the glacier's snout to see the torrent of grey meltwater escaping from beneath the ice. Other longer walks can be undertaken in the park and information on them is available in the warden's office. Skaftafell's campsite is one of the country's best; it is also very popular as many visitors find this the most convenient place from which to look at glaciers. Highly recommended.

Skaftafell's glacial peaks

◆◆
SKÓGAR

There is good farmland below Eyjafjallajökull and many farming communities have prospered here. The history of these local people and their way of life has been kept alive at the charming **folk museum** at Skógar which is well worth visiting. Many of the artefacts have been displayed in traditional turf houses that have themselves been moved to the museum from other localities. Just a short distance from the museum is another of the south's attractions, the 203-foot (62m)-high waterfall of **Skógafoss** which falls like a white curtain against the black rock behind it. Six miles (10km) to the west of Skógar is another waterfall, **Seljalandsfoss**; it doesn't carry much water, but its wispy and windswept features always attract admirers.

◆
SÓLHEIMAJÖKULL

Sólheimajökull, one of Mýrdalsjökull's outlet glaciers, reaches down to within a few kilometres from the ring road

and it is possible to drive a
two-wheel drive vehicle close to
a small glacial river and then
walk along the river bank to
reach the glacier's snout.
The snout is so heavily laden
with rock flour that it is almost
jet black in colour.

◆
VÍK

This small settlement just to the
south of Mýrdalsjökull is
conveniently placed between
the agricultural area around
Selfoss and the popular
stopping place of Skaftafell. A
warning – watch out for arctic
terns near the campsite: when
disturbed they can give a nasty
peck on the head so it may be
wise to wear a hat!

Accommodation
The main places to stay in this
part of Iceland are Vík,
Kirkjubæjarklaustur and Skógar.
Vík has **Hotel Vík** (tel: (98)
71193) and a youth hostel (tel:
(98) 71106) which is to the east
of the settlement.
Kirkjubæjarklaustur has an **Edda
Hotel** (tel: (98) 74799) and there
is also one at Skógar (tel: (98)
78870).
It is very important to remember
that there is very little
accommodation at Skaftafell as it
only has the campsite and the
small guesthouses of **Bölti** (tel:
(97) 81626) and **Freysnes** (tel:
(97) 81845).

Shopping
There are few shops in this part
of Iceland. Vík has the region's
best facilities, though there are
also some in Kirkjubæjarklaustur.
Skaftafell campsite has a
supermarket.

THE EASTERN FIORDS

Eastern Iceland is, geologically
speaking, one of the country's
oldest areas. Long-lost
volcanoes once poured out
copious sheets of lava leaving
behind great thicknesses of
'flood basalts'. After Nature had
spent all that effort building the
mountains, glaciers then
gouged out huge U-shaped
valleys, leaving behind some
very beautiful fiord scenery.
Mountains up to 3,281 feet
(1,000m) high flank the fiords,
many of them with long colourful
scree slopes, such as Stöng in
Berufjördur. The northern-
facing slopes often have cirques
in them as these sides keep
snow and ice much longer than
southern-facing ones; these
scallop-shaped bites out of the
mountains add a touch of
grandeur to the landscape.
This is a rich fishing region and
many of the dozen or so fiords
here have a settlement that has
prospered or declined as the
fish (notably herring) arrived
and left. To make the most of
the sun, settlements were
generally built facing south, but
one, Seydisfjördur, is an
exception to this. The
settlements vary in size and
importance. There are small
ones like **Djúpivogur** that have
their harbour near an exposed
headland and larger ones like
Reyðarfjörður that are
extremely well sheltered and
have safe harbours for larger
ships.
The region's main interest to the
visitor is its fine fiord scenery
rather than particular places of
interest, though of course it is

WHAT TO SEE

Seydisfjördur – almost Scandinavia

well worth spending time in the fishing harbours when boats are bringing in their catches. The northern part of the region (Thistilfjördur, Bakkaflói, Vopnafjördur and Héradsflói) seldom attracts visitors, most of whom are usually too eager to rush towards Mývatn.

◆
EGILSSTADIR
Although Neskaupstadur is the largest settlement in the Eastern Fjords, the region's hub is Egilsstadir, which is not even on the coast. This settlement prospered initially as an important centre for the co-operative movement. The completion of the ring road (on which it stands) and the growing importance of its airport have meant that it now plays a pivotal role in the region's economy.
Egilsstadir stands by the banks of the murky green-coloured **Lagarfljót**, which carries meltwater from Snæfell to the large bay of Héradsflói. This

river flows through **Lögurinn**, one of the country's biggest lakes and reputedly home of a monster. The eastern shore of the lake is wonderfully wooded (by Icelandic standards) and at **Hallormsstadur** there are rich woods as birch and conifers have prospered well in this sheltered area.

◆
HÖFN
This settlement just to the south of the fiords is an important communications centre and for visitors travelling anti-clockwise round the ring road, it is the first sizeable settlement since Selfoss, some 248 miles (400km) away. There is a little **folk museum** (Byggdasfan Austur Skaftfellinga) which is located in a storehouse built in 1864.

◆
SEYDISFJÖRDUR
Since this part of Iceland is the nearest region to the rest of Europe, it is not surprising that other nations, notably the seafaring ones, have had some influence here. This is probably best seen in Seydisfjördur, where many of the older houses have been strongly influenced by Norwegian building styles. The settlement's good harbour and its nearness to the Nordic countries meant that it was a natural choice as the Icelandic port of call for the Faeroese ferry *Norröna*, and the summer sailings of this vessel mean that visitors from afar can bring their vehicles to Iceland.
The settlement itself is certainly worth a visit. It lies at the head of a long curved fiord and the rough mountain pass that links it

to Egilsstadir offers fine views. The pass crosses a barren and windswept tundra plateau that may still have a covering of snow through the summer months. It is used for skiing during the winter.

Accommodation

Visitors will find that there is usually no dearth of places in which to stay when in the Eastern Fiords. At the southern end of the region, Höfn has an **Edda Hotel** (tel: (97) 81470) outside the settlement and within it are the **Hotel Höfn** (tel: (97) 81240) and the youth hostel (tel: (97) 81736). Farther north, the fishing settlements generally have hotels and one that is well known for its cooking is **Hotel Bláfell** (tel: (97) 56770) in Breiddalsvík.

Visitors who are travelling via the ferry *Norröna*, which lands at Seyðisfjördur, may wish to use the settlement's **Hotel Snæfell** (tel: (97) 21460) which is in a very attractive wooden building, or the youth hostel (tel: (97) 21410). Egilsstadir's importance as the region's main communications centre is marked by a number of hotels, the largest being **Hotel Valaskjálf** (tel: (97) 11500); to the north of the settlement, there is the **Edda Hotel** at Eidar (tel: (97) 13803).

Shopping

The Eastern Fiords are well supplied with good shopping facilities. Of the main places visited by tourists, Egilsstadir has very good shops while Höfn, Djúpivogur, Fáskrúdsfjördur and Seydisfjördur are also well served.

MÝVATN AND NORTHEASTERN ICELAND

This is one of the most starkly beautiful areas in all Iceland and its scenery includes huge waterfalls, windswept and barren deserts and, perhaps most fascinating of all, the volcanically active area of Mývatn.

Generally, the region is cooler and drier than the south of the country as the prevailing southwesterly winds have already lost their moisture when they reach the north. However, the influence of cold winds from the Arctic means that the temperatures can be quite cool and snowstorms can occur in July in the higher areas. By comparison, in sheltered areas pleasant sunshine can bring the temperature up to 25°C (75°F) or more – not bad for only 1 degree below the Arctic Circle! The section of the ring road that runs from Egilsstadir to Mývatn passes through a vast wind-

An arctic summer night, Húsavik

swept desert and the journey here can be tremendously exciting in good weather but unpleasant in bad conditions. The desert is generally quite bare with little plant life in evidence; the land has been inundated with ash from the volcanoes that lie to the south and also periodically flooded by the great glacial rivers of Jökulsá á Brú and Jökulsá á Fjöllum.

The **Jökulsá á Brú** has huge moraines by its banks and rather surprisingly, a few farms are found here. Farther west, there are two small patches of agricultural land which are veritable oases in this wilderness at **Mödrudalur** and **Grímsstadir**. At an altitude of 1,538 feet (469m), Mödrudalur is the highest farm in the country. To the south of the ring road, a bare gravel, ash and lava-covered plain extends towards the interior. The well known mountain of **Herdubreid** 5,518 feet (1682m) is an easily recognised landmark – it is a steep-sided table mountain with a volcanic cone on its summit, making it look very much like a circus big top. There are also views towards Vatnajökull and Dyngjufjöll.

◆◆
HÚSAVÍK

Húsavík is a busy fishing settlement in the wide bay of Skjálfandi; it also has good shopping facilities. There is an interesting church on the main street built with Norwegian timber, and the settlement's **folk museum** (Safnahúsid Stórigardur) has a (now stuffed!)

polar bear that landed on the island of Grímsey in 1969, presumably after it had been carried over from Greenland on an ice floe.

As Húsavík is less than 38 miles (60km) from the Arctic Circle, the settlement is conveniently situated for visitors wanting to see the midnight sun from the northern peninsula of Tjornes. This peninsula is well known for its fossil beds at **Ytritunga**, indicators of Iceland's warmer climate a rather long time ago.

◆◆◆
JÖKULSÁRGLJÚFUR NATIONAL PARK

The big river of **Jökulsá á Fjöllum** flows from the northern edge of Vatnajökull all the way to the Arctic Ocean, a distance of some 127 miles (206km). The river's starting point is in the ice caves at **Kverkfjöll**, a stopping point for tour buses. The river carries a huge mass of sediment and has helped build up a large area of gravelly desert along its route. It has also drastically changed the landscape by creating the huge canyon of **Jökulsárgljúfur** and many of the river's best waterfalls lie in the Jökulsárgljúfur National Park. The park's best known feature is **Dettifoss** and at 147 feet (45m) high it is Europe's most powerful waterfall. The grey river thunders over this, sending a huge cloud of spray up into the air. The smaller, but very fine, waterfall of **Hafragilsfoss** is farther downstream.

Rivers continually change their route and the Jökulsá á Fjöllum is no exception; one previous route was probably through the

Jökulsárgljúfur's grand canyon

horseshoe-shaped canyon of **Ásbyrgi**, a strangely-shaped bite out of the landscape that has vertical cliffs some 200 feet (60m) high. Viking legends claim that it was made by one of the hoofs of Sleipnir, Óđin's horse.

Just upstream of Ásbyrgi is **Vesturdalur**, where the river has eroded the basalt rocks to reveal countless numbers of basalt columns at **Hljodaklettar**. This is natural sculpture at its best – three-dimensional fans of rock indicate the intricate cooling patterns that developed within the hot rock after it solidified.

◆◆◆
MÝVATN

Lake Mývatn is the jewel of northern Iceland. Set high up between the hills, with cold deserts and lavafields nearby, the district around the lake has perhaps the most varied scenery in all Iceland.

Lavaflows of various ages can be seen near the lake, the most recent ones (1981–84) coming from a hill to the northeast, **Leirhnjúkur**. This series of eruptions are known as the 'Krafla Fires' after the local mountain **Krafla**, and these followed the 'Mývatn Fires' of 1724–29 which also flowed from the Krafla area. Some of these earlier lavaflows can be seen beside the lake's northern shore and within the lake's main settlement of **Reykjahlíd.** The settlement's main campsite is situated beside the lavafield and tents are often pitched in the very sheltered spots between the huge domes of lava. Nearer the lakeside, the lava actually encircled the local church without harming it. The area around Leirhnjúkur is still active, with vapour and sulphurous gases rising from the hot rocks. There is the very real possibility that more eruptions may happen in the near future.

Tourists regularly wander over

the new lava, exploring the frozen lava 'rivers' and looking down from crater rims to the tongues of black lava. Crevices in the new rock may have sulphur deposits or even small plants that have somehow managed to colonise this inhospitable environment. A visit to Leirhnjúkur is highly recommended but great care must be taken when exploring the new lavafield.

Just to the east of Leirhnjúkur stands the crater lake of **Víti** ('Hell') which has a rim 1,049 feet (320m) in diameter; this was where the Mývatn Fires started and it was the site of a boiling mud pool for 100 years. The road up to Leirhnjúkur passes the Krafla geothermal power station. This large and complex installation only produces electricity during the winter when demand is high. During the summer engineers are kept busy drilling more boreholes into the flanks of Krafla and tapping the steam that is produced when rainwater percolates down through the lava to the hot rocks below. Iceland's best known area of mudpools and solfatara activity is at **Hverarond**, just to the east of Mývatn. Large blue-grey pools full of hot bubbling mud slurp away to the delight of onlookers. The pools spit out globules of mud, some of them building spatter cones about 3 feet (1m) high round their rims. Hverarond sits below the hill of **Námafjall** which was the site of sulphur mining.

To the east of the lake are the crater rows of **Threngslaborgir** and **Lúdentsborgir**. About 2,000

years ago they sent out streams of lava towards the lake. At one stage of the activity, a large lava lake was formed, a pond of red-hot rock swirling about under the influence of strong convection currents. Gradually, parts of this lake cooled, forming solid lava columns and after a sudden emptying of the lake these were left *in situ* as tall twisted towers of lava. These remarkable formations

are preserved in the park known as **Dimmuborgir** ('Black Castles'). When the lava from the two crater rows continued flowing towards the lake, it flowed over waterlogged land. The hot lava turned the trapped water into superheated steam which then exploded its way upwards through the congealing lava. This process left behind 'pseudocraters', so-called because no lava ever flowed out of them, and dozens of these craters are found round the lake and on the lake's islands. Iceland has many volcanoes with large craters, but perhaps the most intriguing of them all is **Hverfjall**, just to the east of the lake. This ash cone stands 534 feet (163m) above ground level and has a smaller cone within its large crater. The eruption that formed Hverfjall took place about 2,500 years ago and may

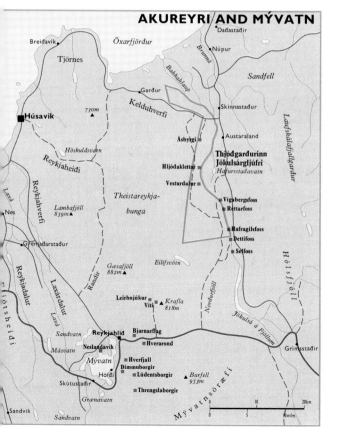

AKUREYRI AND MÝVATN

have lasted less than one day. Much of the Mývatn area is quite devoid of trees, but on the eastern shore's promontory of **Höfði** visitors will find a wonderfully wooded little park that has a rich display of trees, shrubs and flowers. This overlooks a small bay in which there are tall red-coloured lava columns that were formed at the same time as Dimmuborgir's. Just to the east of the lake is **Bjarnarflag** beneath which is a powerful source of geothermal energy. Bjarnaflag is the site of a diatomite factory which uses natural steam to process the lakebed's diatomaceous sediment into filtering materials. A short distance from the factory, the warm ground supports a few small fields of potatoes which grow remarkably well in the otherwise completely barren ground.

But there is another side to the natural wonders of Mývatn – the birds. The lake's proximity to a volcanically active area means that a number of warm springs (at temperatures up to 41°C/105°F) flow into the north-eastern corner of the lake, keeping that part of it ice-free during the winter. Also, with the lake being so shallow (up to 13 feet (4m) deep), there is more than enough light getting to the lake bed to help provide a vast amount of nutrients. The lake supports a duck population that is counted in tens of thousands at the height of the breeding season. Breeds such as tufted duck, scaup and wigeon are all found here, but the duck most sought-after by European bird-watchers is Barrow's goldeneye.

Iceland is its only European home. Another interesting duck is the harlequin, which can be seen in the fast-flowing **Laxá**, the outlet of the lake which takes its water to the northern bay of Skjálfandi. Whooper swans can be seen in the western bay of Neslandavík and some ponds near the lake may have great northern divers. The birds' main breeding area is to the west and northwest of the lake and access to it is restricted during the early part of the summer. The ducks eat the fish that live in the lake and also, thankfully, the local midges – and there are countless millions of these little beasts. Ominously, Mývatn means 'midge lake'! These can be incredibly annoying when they swarm, so safety (and sanity) can be sought in windier places. Fortunately, they do not bite – but watch out for the blackfly that live by the southern shore, they do!

Accommodation

Mývatn is served by two hotels, **Hotel Reynihlíd** (tel: (96) 44170) and **Hotel Reykjahlíd** (tel: (96) 44142), both of which are in the settlement of Reykjahlíd. Húsavík's main hotel is **Hotel Húsavík** (tel: (96) 41220) and there are some places to stay in the northeast of the region, for example, **Guesthouse K.N.P.** (tel: (96) 52121) in Kópasker.

Shopping

The region's main centre for shopping is Húsavík. There are two small supermarkets at Mývatn: at Reykjahlíd (at the northeastern corner) and at Skútustadir (by the southern shore).

AKUREYRI AND NORTHERN ICELAND

Northern Iceland contains a great variety of scenery including big mountains, rich farmland and a long rugged coastline. The mainstay of much of the northern economy is farming and the area around Skagafjördur is renowned for the horses that are bred there. A few fishing settlements are found on the northern peninsulas, for example Siglufjördur and Ólafsfjördur, but these are not as prosperous as their counterparts in other regions of the country.

The ring road only meets a few settlements on its journey through a series of important mountain passes.

◆◆
AKUREYRI

Akureyri, which is on the western shore of Eyjafördur, is the capital of northern Iceland. This is the country's third largest town after Reykjavík and Kópavogur (the capital's neighbour) and is a bustling place with shipyards, factories, important transport links and a good shopping centre, making it the economic hub of the region.

But all this industry does not spoil the town. Akureyri is set within a rich farming area below high mountains and its streets are lined with countless trees. As a mark of just how fertile the land is, the town has excellent **Botanic Gardens** ('Lystigardur Akureyrar') that were founded by the townswomen in 1912. There is a huge collection of plants here, ranging from the humble dandelion (yes, it is an exhibit!) to mature trees. (*Open*: Monday to Friday 08.00–22.00hrs, Saturday and Sunday 09.00–22.00hrs.) Elsewhere in the town, Livingstone daisies (an African plant) can be seen in full colour during the summer months.

Akureyri's colourful roofs

The oldest part of Akureyri lies between the town centre and the airfield. Look out for some charming wooden houses, some of which have rich associations with Icelandic literature.
Sigurhæðir (at Eyrarlandsvegur 3, built in 1902) was the home of the poet Matthías Jochumsson. *Open*: daily in summer 14.00–16.00hrs. **Nonnahús** (at Aðalstræti 54, built in 1849) was the childhood home of the writer Jón Sveinsson, whose pen name was 'Nonni' and who left Iceland at the age of 12 when he was given the chance of an education in France.
He revisited Iceland only twice, but his deep nostalgia for his boyhood home is revealed in the children's books he wrote. *Open*: daily in summer 14.00–16.30hrs. **Davíðshús** (Bjarkarstígur 6, built in 1944) was the home of the writer Davíð Stefánsson. *Open*: daily in summer 15.00–17.00hrs.
Minjasafnid, the Akureyri Museum, is at Aðalstræti 58 and contains many artefacts dealing with farming, fishing and traditional crafts. *Summer opening*: daily 13.30–17.00hrs. *Winter opening*: Sunday 14.00–16.00hrs. *Closed*: Monday to Saturday.
Náttúrugripasafnid (The Museum of Natural History) is at Hafnarstræti 81 and has collections of birds, eggs, rocks and plants.
Summer opening: Sunday to Friday 13.00–16.00hrs. *Closed*: Saturday. *Winter opening*: Sunday 13.00–15.00hrs. *Closed*: Monday to Saturday.
The **Akureyri church** sits in a

Lystigardur Akureyrar

prominent position above the shopping area and is the town's most distinctive building. One of its stained glass windows came from the old Coventry Cathedral in England. *Open*: daily 09.30–11.00hrs and 14.00–15.30hrs.

◆
BLÖNDUÓS
Blönduós is an important trading settlement on the eastern shore of Húnaflói and is the only settlement of size between Akureyri and Borgarnes, a distance of over 180 miles (300km). It has a **handicrafts museum** ('Heimilisidnadarsafnid').

◆
GODAFOSS
The waterfall's name ('Falls of the Gods') celebrates the event in AD1000 when Thorgeir, Lawspeaker at the Althing

which had decided in favour of the adoption of Christianity, threw his pagan idols into the river **Skálfandafljót**.

This important river flows from Vatnajökull and drains the western side of the huge lavafield of **Ódáðahraun**. A road follows the western bank of the river upstream to the farm of **Mýri** and from there a track (for four-wheel drive vehicles only) leads to the cross-country route across **Sprengisandur**. The fine waterfall of **Aldeyjarfoss** is reached from this track only a few kilometres from the farm; it is well worth the walk.

To the west of Goðafoss lies the long valley of **Fnjóskadalur** and on its eastern side is the richly wooded area of **Vaglaskógur**. The woods give an indication of what many parts of Iceland must have looked like around the time of the Settlement and before deforestation began.

◆
GRÍMSEY

This small island north of Akureyri sits astride the Arctic Circle. It is connected to Akureyri by sea and air and is of great interest to birdwatchers, being home to kittiwakes, Brünnich's guillemots, fulmars and razorbills; one very interesting bird found here is the rare little auk.

To the northwest of Grímsey lies the rocky outpost of **Kolbeinsey**. It may only be a dot on a map but it is vitally important to the Icelanders as the boundaries of their territorial waters are based on the position of this rock – as long as it is above the sea! Unfortunately, it is crumbling away and has been patched up with concrete to safeguard the boundary!

◆
HÓLAR

Although Hólar is remote from today's centres of population, it was once the seat of the bishops of northern Iceland from 1106 to 1789. The best known bishops were Jón Arason (1522–1550), who was beheaded at Skálholt and Guðbrandur Thorláksson (1571–1627) who was the first Icelander to make a map of the country.

The present church is a well built structure dating back to 1763. The tall bell tower beside it was erected in 1950.

◆
VARMAHLÍÐ

This little settlement on the ring road is a convenient stopping point when travelling through northern Iceland. It is in the

WHAT TO SEE

important horse-breeding area of Skagafjördur and pony trekking is available from farms in the district.

Just a few kilometres to the north of Varmahlíd is the old farmhouse of **Glaumbær** which is now a museum. This is a very interesting place to visit as the substantial building is fully furnished and has lots of farmhouse implements; the kitchen and pantry are in the style of the 18th century. The outside walls of the building are constructed with large sods of turf which are arranged in a very neat pattern.

The small wooden church at **Vidimyri** is only a few kilometres west of Varmahlíd, this small building was built in 1834 and has a turf roof.

Accommodation

Akureyri has numerous hotels and guesthouses and there are also places to stay on the outskirts of the town. Within Akureyri, the best known places are **Hotel Edda** (tel: (96) 24055),

Glaumbær's old wooden farm house is now a museum

Hotel KEA (tel: (96) 22200) and **Hotel Nordurland** (tel: (96) 22600). There are two youth hostels, one in the town (tel: (96) 23657) and one just to the north of it (tel: (96) 25037).

In the west of the region, there is accommodation in Varmahlíd at **Hotel Varmahlíd** (tel: (95) 6170/38170) and farther west still in Blönduós at **Hotel Blönduós** (tel: (95) 24126) and in Saudárkrókur at **Hotel Áning** (tel: (95) 36717).

Shopping

Akureyri is a really good place in which to shop and many visitors will take advantage of its wide variety of shops and services. One place of note in the town is the Álafoss **woollen mill's factory shop** which is found in the industrial estate on the southern bank of the Glerá. Given the size of the population, you will be surprised at the remarkable number of bookshops.

Much farther west, Saudárkrókur and Blönduós have reasonable shopping facilities; Varmahlíd has a supermarket, so stock up while you can.

SNÆFELLSNES AND THE WEST

This region is made up of the prominent peninsula of Snæfellsnes and the area around the fiords of Borgarfjördur and Hvalfjörður. Snæfellsnes's position, jutting into the Atlantic Ocean, means that it is dominated by the sea. The northern communities of Stykkishólmur, Grundarfjördur and Ólafsvík are important fishing settlements. Scallop fishing is very important in some places and the scallop shells are so numerous that these are sometimes used instead of gravel to make paths and tracks; fish farming has also been started in the area.

The ice-capped volcano of Snæfellsjökull dominates the landscape in this part of the country. This beautifully-shaped conical mountain has erupted on numerous occasions, spewing out ashes and lava over much of western Snæfellsnes. The volcano's name may be familiar to many visitors as it was here that Jules Verne's intrepid travellers started their long journey of discovery in *Journey to the Centre of the Earth*. After exploring the bowels of the Earth, they emerged at Stromboli, a volcano on an island off the southern tip of Italy!

The large lavafields that surround Snæfellsjökull, especially to its south and southwest, have inhibited settlements being established; but the coast is home to many seabirds, for example at Arnarstapi.

The area between Borgarfjördur and Húsafell contains a great many farms, a number of which have glasshouses in which geothermally-heated water is used by the owners to bring the crops on.

◆
AKRANES

Akranes is an industrial town and its tall chimney marks the whereabouts of the country's only cement factory. All the raw materials (shell sand, basalt sand and rhyolite) are found locally.

The two main reasons for visiting Akranes are its connection by regular ferry service to Reykjavík and the interesting **museum**. The museum ('Byggdasafnid') has many exhibits including an old trading ship. Outside the building is a tall monument with text written in Icelandic and Gaelic. It was a gift from the people of Ireland in 1974, the 1100th anniversary of the Settlement. It celebrates the district's original settlers who came from Ireland around AD880.

To the east of Akranes is the long curved fiord of **Hvalfjörður** ('Whale Fiord'). As the name suggests, this has an association with whaling and the whaling station at the head of the fiord ceased production only in the late 1980s after much international debate about the future of this controversial industry. The fiord has very deep anchorages; these made it an ideal base for large numbers of British and US naval ships during World War II.

Fishing boats at Grundarfjördur

◆◆
ARNARSTAPI

If people have found living conditions difficult in Snæfellsnes, then the seabirds have found them most attractive. The sea has carved out tall cliff faces, sea stacks and skerries that are all havens to countless birds. Kittiwakes are numerous and birdwatchers will be thrilled at the sight of so many birds in such beautiful scenery. A tall sculpture of the mythical figure Bárdur Snæfellsnes, who lived in Snæfellsjökull, stands near the middle of this small settlement.

◆
BORGARNES

This settlement in Borgarfjördur is unusual in that although it is on the coast, it is not reliant on fishing for its livelihood. Instead, it is an important service centre for the surrounding agricultural area.

There is a little park in the middle of the settlement and in it a burial mound thought to be that of Skallagrímur Kveldúlfsson, the district's first settler. Almost next to it, a large plaque depicts Skallagrímur's son Egill Skallagrímsson carrying home the body of his drowned son, Bödvar. The town has a museum ('Safnahús Borgarfjardar') with art and natural history collections.

◆
FLATEY

This is the only inhabited island in Breidafjördur. An important trading centre in the Middle Ages, today only about 40 people live here permanently, though many houses have been renovated for summer use. The car ferry *Baldur* calls at Flatey as it crosses from Stykkishólmur to Brjánslækur and during the crossing there are superb opportunities for studying the many seabirds that live in this very large island-studded bay.

The island gave its name to *Flateyjarbók*, which was written about 1390. This was the biggest of the early Icelandic books and it contains the *Saga of Kings* (that is, of Norway). This was a work of craftsmanship as well as one of literature. Its 225 leaves needed a total of 113 calfskins to produce it.

◆◆
HÚSAFELL

The farm of Húsafell is now a recreation area based on a popular campsite in a little birch wood. It is right at the eastern edge of the region's farming area and the uninhabited interior is tantalisingly close. This is a particularly good place for keen walkers to visit.

To the south of Húsafell, a rough track through the high pass known as **Kaldidalur** heads towards Thingvallavatn. Although this is 'officially' a track, it is often negotiable by two-wheel drive vehicles in the height of summer though care is needed as the surface can be loose and there are steep hills. This route travels over a barren tundra plateau and gives superb views of the ice-cap **Thórisjökull**. To Húsafell's northeast lies the lavafield of **Hallmundarhraun** which can be reached by a four-wheel drive vehicle. Iceland's most famous lava cave, **Surtshellir**, lies below the surface and this is quite an enormous structure – one cavern in it is some 82 feet (25m) high and 65 feet (20m) wide. The entrance to the cave is through the collapsed roof and great care must be taken on entering it as the floor is strewn with fallen boulders. Lava 'tide marks', indicating the levels of the 'lava rivers', can be seen. This place is fascinating but potentially dangerous, so don't go in alone and anyone entering it must have a good torch.

The river **Hvítá** ('White River') runs to the west of Húsafell and downstream of the farm can be found the very unusual water-falls known as **Hraunfossar**. Here, the river skirts the edge of a lavafield and the water level is many metres below the top surface of the lavafield. At the lava's edge, the water gushes out of the porous rock and falls into the river, this water's crystal-clear purity being in great contrast to the murky glacial water of the Hvítá.

◆
REYKHOLT

Reykholt's claim to fame is that this was the home of Snorri Sturluson – statesman, politician, warrior and writer; there seems to have been no end to this versatile but notorious man's talents. The only tangible remains of his house is the small circular pool in which he used to bathe. This little pool of warm water (called 'Snorralaug') was reached by a still extant passageway that ran from the farmhouse and it was possibly in this confined space that he was trapped and stabbed to death in 1241.

Reykholt consists of a large Edda Hotel, two churches and a handful of houses. The older church has a gravestone marked *Sturlungareitur* and this may be where Snorri is buried.

WHAT TO SEE

◆◆
STYKKISHÓLMUR

This is a very pleasant settlement on the north coast and the base for the ferry *Baldur* which sails to Brjánslækur in the Northwest Fiords. This has been a trading post for some time and close to the harbour stands the 'Norwegian House' which was built in 1829 and is now used as a museum. However, the most striking building in the settlement is the new Roman Catholic church, a tall concrete structure with long graceful lines that sweep upwards in gentle curves.

The settlement has many connections with the Sagas and nearby, the little hill of **Helgafell** features in the saga of the local area, called *Eyrbyggjasaga*. According to old tales, no-one with an unwashed face was allowed to look at it and those who climbed it without looking back or talking had three

Helgafell – the magic mountain

wishes granted. It is an easily reached viewpoint, so make your wishes!

Accommodation

Akranes' main hotel is **Hotel Ósk** (tel: (93) 13314) and in the north of the Snæfellsnes peninsula, the main place to stay is Stykkishólmur which has a youth hostel (tel: (93) 81095) and **Hotel Stykkishólmur** (tel: (93) 81330). To the south of the peninsula, a convenient place to halt is **Hotel Búðir** (tel: (93) 56700). Borgarnes has **Hotel Borgarnes** (tel: (93) 71119) and in the east of the region, there is an **Edda Hotel** at Reykholt (tel: (51260) and a large youth hostel at Varmaland (tel: (93) 51301).

Shopping

Akranes has good shopping facilities with a wide range of shops and services. Borgarnes and Stykkishólmur both have quite reasonable shops while there are rather fewer facilities in the settlements of Grundarfjörður and Ólafsvík.

THE NORTHWEST FIORDS

The region known as the Northwest Fiords is essentially a very large peninsula that is indented by a myriad of fiords – all of them quite different in character. Only a small number of the fiords are inhabited as there is very little farming land available and the population is rather sparse, even for Iceland. The region is also subjected to cruelly-cold Arctic winds, another factor making life difficult. In summer, however, the region can be quite beautiful, with the dark basalt mountains towering above the deep blue water of the fiords. Cirques (or corries or cwms) grace many of the fiords; these were carved out of the basalt mountains by solitary glaciers and today they look like armchairs that were fashioned for giants – or was it trolls?

It is fishing that keeps people alive in the region; the land is so poor and the climate so harsh that only the rich harvest from the sea keeps these communities viable.

However, after every really harsh winter, more people take the decision to move to the capital where the winter is rather more bearable.

Only the coastal fringes are inhabited. In the mountainous central part of the region lies a desolate high tundra plateau – the wasteland of Gláma. This is a large expanse of frost-shattered boulders, moraines and lakes that has only recently been deglaciated. A number of roads cross the edge of this unhabitable area.

The western side of the region has a number of small settlements, a number of them sited on sandy spits of land jutting into the fiords. These include Patreksfjördur, Tálknafjördur, Bíldudalur, Thingeyri, Flateyri and Bolungarvík. Each has its own little harbour and local fishing boats that maintain the life of the community.

Not very many visitors venture up to this region as this is rather far from the 'traditional' tourist routes near the ring road and the distances between settlements are, by Icelandic standards, quite far. For example, although Ísafjördur and Patreksfjördur are only 37 miles (66km) apart as the crow flies, the road distance is some 116 miles (189km) as the route weaves in and out of the fiords. Two boat services that may be of interest are the car ferry *Baldur* that sails daily between Brjánslækur and Stykkishólmur (across the bay of Breidarfjördur) and the regular sailings of the *Fagranes* from Ísafjördur to Hornstrandir and a few places in Ísafjardardjúp.

◆◆
HORNSTRANDIR

The Northwest Fiords are split into two main sections by the long fiord of Ísafjardardjúp and to the east of this lies the ice-cap **Drangajökull**. To the northwest of the ice-cap lies the uninhabited area known as Hornstrandir which is now protected as a nature reserve. This is the very tip of European civilisation. Until the 1950s, the area was inhabited by a few

WHAT TO SEE

farmers who managed to eke out a living but finally even they could no longer sustain a livelihood in this cold outpost. Not even sheep roam in Hornstrandir, so the wild flowers grow ungrazed, welcoming the walkers and campers that venture into this haven of peace. There are no roads to this area, so visitors must reach it by boat (the *Fagranes*) from Ísafjördur.

◆
HRAFNSEYRI

This is a small farm on the northern coast of Arnarfjördur which was the birthplace in 1811 of the Icelandic patriot Jón Sigurdsson. There are a few remains of the house in which he was born and there is also a museum and a chapel dedicated to him. A charming little church of 1886 stands nearby.

◆◆
ÍSAFJÖRDUR

This is the region's main settlement and it dates back to the 18th century. Today, this is a lively fishing port, connected to Reykjavík by frequent flights. One fascinating place to visit is the **Maritime Museum** which is found near the tip of the L-shaped spit of land that juts into the fiord. This museum consists of four buildings that were built between 1736 and 1785 and which contain a wide variety of artefacts associated with the fishing industry; well worth visiting.

◆◆
LATRABJARG

While people find the region

Hrafnseyri, on the coast of Arnafjördur

difficult to prosper in, the cliffs and skerries around the shore are havens for birdlife. The most spectacular bird cliffs are at Latrabjarg, at the western tip of the region. The cliffs here are about 7 miles (12km) long and range between 1,300 and 1,600 feet (400-500m) high; they are home to countless seabirds including razorbills and Brünnich's guillemots.

For centuries, local men have scaled the cliffs to collect eggs and birds. These provided food, oil for lighting and feathers for clothing and quilts. While these daredevil skills are no longer relied on for making ends meet, they were invaluable when the British trawler *Dhoon* ran aground in 1947. One by one, each and every crew member of the stricken ship was hauled up these gigantic cliffs, a rescue

that went down in the history books of this great seafaring nation.

Accommodation

In Ísafjördur, **Hotel Ísafjörður** (tel: (94) 4111) is handily placed for touring the area. To its east (and near the head of Ísafjardardjúp) there is the large **Hotel Reykjanes** (tel: (94) 4844). A number of settlements on the western coast have accommodation available. Anyone visiting the cliffs at Latrabjarg may wish to stay at the youth hostel at Breidavík (tel: (94) 1575), while on the southern coast there is **Hotel Flókalundur** (tel: (94) 2011) which is only a few kilometres east of Brjánslækur, destination of the ferry *Baldur*.

Shopping

Ísafjördur has very good shopping facilities and the fishing settlements around the coast also have shops.

THE INTERIOR

The interior of Iceland is dominated by the great ice-caps of Vatnajökull, Langjökull and Hofsjökull. For countless years, these huge ice masses have accumulated ice and then slipped it down icy 'tongues', ripping up the land in the process. Hundreds of grey-coloured glacial rivers take much of the ground-down waste to the sea, but in the interior lies the debris of earlier times when the ice-caps were even bigger and spread their influence over a larger area. Today, the interior is largely a huge grey desert covered with sand, gravel and frost-shattered boulders. In most areas, the land is quite barren, save for a few hardy plants that somehow manage to obtain water in this dry and dusty environment. Tall mountains, often jagged, pierce this undulating mass of grey; the general altitude is about 1,600-3,000 feet (500-900m), with the summits of the ice-caps above 4,300 feet (1,300m). No-one lives in the interior, save a few hardy souls working at the meteorological station at Hveravellir. Since the area is covered with snow for most of the year, the tracks through the interior may be open for only a couple of months each summer and a four-wheel drive vehicle is definitely needed to negotiate these routes. During the autumn, the farmers must come up to the highlands to round up their sheep – a daunting task considering the vast open spaces. Transport in the winter is by snowcat or skiddoo – the

WHAT TO SEE

latter is a very popular mode of transport with more robust types.

The glacial and non-glacial rivers that radiate from the ice-caps and the mountain ranges have long been obstacles to travel through the interior. It is a hard enough job to cross the land today so goodness knows what it must have been like in earlier times; ponies, no matter how sure-footed, do not travel as quickly as four-wheel drive vehicles! There are only a few safe cross-country routes through the interior. The two north/south ones are called **Kjölur** (which runs between Langjökull and Hofsjökull) and **Sprengisandur** (which runs between Hofsjökull and Vatnajökull). Another popular route is through the Fjallabak Nature Reserve (round the northeastern side of Mýrdalsjökull).

For many visitors, a journey through the wilderness of the interior is the highlight of their holiday. On a good summer day the desert can be warm and the panoramic views of the mountains and the ice-caps are sights that will be treasured forever. However, it has to be remembered that in poor weather there is almost nothing to see and one cold desert looks very much like another.

Visitors to the interior may come across places associated with the 18th-century outlaw Fjalla-Eyvindur. He and his wife Halla were banished into the interior for the crime of killing a child and they survived an incredible 20 years in this wilderness. Robinson Crusoe had it easy compared to the problems faced by this couple – deserts, lavafields, sparse vegetation, very little food available, hardly any drinking water, and snow for much of the year. At Herdubreidarlindir they built a little hut over a stream and this can still be seen, and at Hveravellir they erected a hideout close to the hot spring area where they could do their cooking.

♦♦♦
ASKJA

Just to the north of Vatnajökull is the mountain range known as the **Dyngjufjöll** and to its north is the **Ódáðahraun** ('Desert of Misdeeds') to which outlaws were banished.

In 1875, farmers in the Mývatn area noticed clouds of smoke and ash coming from the Dyngjufjöll. A brave group undertook the difficult journey to the area to see what was happening. A massive eruption had taken place, with some of the pumice that was ejected forming rafts on the open sea; even farther away, some of the ash had landed in Stockholm! In the centre of the Dyngjufjöll, a massive caldera had been formed (this is a depression caused by the land sinking after an eruption) and it was named Askja. This now contains the lake **Óskjuvatn** and just by its northern shore lies the crater **Víti** ('Hell') in which visitors can bathe in its still-warm water – even though it has a rather strong sulphurous smell. There was an eruption in Askja in 1961 and this lava must be driven over in order to reach Óskjuvatn and Víti.

The route to Askja follows the eastern side of the great glacial river of **Jökulsá á Fjöllum** and passes **Herdubreid** ('Broad Shoulder'), one of the country's most beautiful mountains. The track skirts the small oasis of **Herdubreidarlindir** where a stream of crystal-clear water passes through the rich vegetation. Tour buses visit Askja and this trip is highly recommended.

Under the volcano – the vast lake of Öskjuvatn

◆◆◆
ELDGJÁ

Many of Iceland's volcanic eruptions have taken place through fissures and Eldgjá ('Fire Gorge') which is to the northeast of Mýrdalsjökull is the world's largest fissure. In total, it is some 11 miles (18km) long, about 1,640 feet (500m) wide and 500 feet (150m) deep. The fissure's greatest attraction is not its size, nor its red-coloured lip, but a very special waterfall called **Ófærufoss** that tumbles into it. This is a double waterfall and what makes it so special and unique is its natural arch above the second fall. It is wide enough to walk across if you do not suffer from vertigo!

◆◆◆
HVERAVELLIR

As the interior is essentially one vast cold desert, this oasis comes as a very pleasant surprise. With its hot springs, a geyser and bathers happily soaking in natural warm water, Hveravellir lies right in the middle of the country on the Kjölur route. It can be very busy at times as it is quite a remarkable place, especially as there are views of both Langjökull and Hofsjökull from it. Very welcoming; well worth a visit.

WHAT TO SEE

Hveravellir: springs and a geyser

The **Kerlingarfjöll** mountains stand to the southeast of Hveravellir and these jagged and colourful peaks provide summer skiing. The valley of Árskardsá is where the ski centre is situated and it has a geothermal source of energy.

◆◆◆
LANDMANNALAUGAR
While much of the interior (and, indeed, most of the country) is based on grey basalt, Landmannalaugar's hills are made of rhyolite, a rock that erodes to form colourful scree slopes. The rhyolite owes its presence to the very strong geothermal source at Torfajökull, to the south of Landmannalaugar. The most obvious result of this activity is that the rocks are vividly coloured – oranges, greens, yellows, reds, creams, and browns – making this quite a photographer's dream. The tourist hut at Landmannalaugar sits beside a lavafield that has a stream of warm water running from beneath its interior and this is sensibly utilised in a communal bath. Great fun! The area around Landmannalaugar is within the Fjallabak National Park. Highly recommended.

Accommodation
Apart from the tourist huts in the interior, the only place to stay is **Hotel Versalir** (tel: (98) 75078) near the southern end of the Sprengisandur route.

Shopping
Anyone venturing into the interior must carry all their provisions with them as there are no shops, petrol stations or any other shopping facilities – so be prepared!

PEACE AND QUIET

Wildlife and Countryside in Iceland
by Paul Sterry

Iceland is a country of great natural beauty. Born of fire and moulded by ice and water, it is a land where the forces of nature have left their mark. Active volcanoes remain to this day and the landscape bears witness to the pent-up energy beneath the surface: hot water geysers, sulphur vents, pools of boiling mud and vast deserts of ash are on most visitors' itineraries. Evidence of glaciation, past and present, is also everywhere, a reminder of the influence that ice has had, and continues to have, on the landscape.

Visitors soon discover a more subtle side to Iceland. Tundra mosses and lichens have softened the appearance of many lavafields, while birch woodlands and lush, wetland vegetation grow along the coast. Considering Iceland's proximity to the Arctic Circle, many visitors are surprised by its floral variety: the warm waters of the Gulf Stream have a profound influence on the climate and vegetation.

The wetlands and tundra are a haven for breeding birds, the comparatively small number of species being more than made up for by the size of their populations. Vast numbers of wildfowl and waders can be seen during spring and summer, most migrating south before the onset of winter.

A reduction in the natural woodland and the creation of hay meadows are two notable features of modern Iceland. Although the inhospitable nature of the terrain and the small population effectively safeguards much of Iceland's wildlife and scenery, three national parks and several designated areas protect the most vulnerable places.

Reykjavík

A surprising amount of wildlife can be seen in and around Reykjavík. Leafy gardens, often overgrown with sweet cicely – a charming relative of cow parsley with a very strong smell of aniseed – are home to nesting redwings. These handsome thrushes spend the summer in Iceland then migrate down into mainland Europe, where they are harbingers of winter.

In the heart of the city, Lake Tjörnin is a good spot to study wildfowl, many of which are rather tame. The waterfront near the Parliament building is worth checking for gulls. Outside the city, almost any stretch of shoreline is worth exploring. Various species of

Redwing and nestlings

PEACE AND QUIET

wader, including redshanks, oystercatchers and ringed plovers feed among the seaweed, and are joined by turnstones, whimbrels and purple sandpipers outside the breeding season. The coast at Stokkseyri is particularly good because the nearby coastal pools may have whooper swans and red-necked phalaropes, dainty little waders which have perfected role reversal – he incubates the eggs and looks after the chicks.

The Reykjanes peninsula is worth visiting for its seabird cliffs: Krísuríkurberg and Hafnaberg support five species of auks, as well as gulls.

Fresh water

Iceland's perimeter is dotted with marshes, pools, lakes and rivers. At certain times of year, visitors might be forgiven for thinking that the wildlife is entirely represented by the midges and biting flies that often abound. However, these wetland habitats are vital breeding grounds for waders and wildfowl.

Inaccessible islands on some pools may harbour whooper swans, while on large lakes, great northern divers can be found. The mournful, wailing call of these birds is one of the most characteristic sounds of Iceland. It is a sound you should try to hear; once you have, you will never forget it.

Agricultural Land

In one respect at least, the Icelander's effect on his environment has enhanced wildlife diversity. Hay meadows and smallholdings are bright with colourful spring flowers before cutting time and are the haunt of large numbers of breeding waders.

Look for flowers of yellow rattle, eyebright, meadowsweet, dandelion, hawkweed, lady's bedstraw, harebells, and wild angelica and among the rich growth of grass. Starlings are common around buildings, and other nesting species include black-tailed godwits, snipe, redshanks and dunlins.

Yellow marsh saxifrage

Tundra

As lavaflows age and weather,
they become colonised by
mosses and lichens. At first, the
vegetation may be confined to
sheltered crevices and holes
but with time it forms a
blanketing carpet; walking
across this tundra heathland
habitat is like walking on
sponge.

Once the mosses and lichens
have established a hold on the
rocky terrain, other plants can
soon follow. Clubmosses, ferns,
and finally dwarf shrubs and
trees appear: bearberry,
crowberry, bog whortleberry,
dwarf birch and several species
of willow are widespread.
Reindeer moss – in fact a lichen,
not a moss – and woolly fringed
moss are the most characteristic
plants of the tundra, but in
localised areas a thorough
search should reveal a variety of
flowering plants as well. Among
the more interesting are several
species of orchid.

Volcanic Activity

There are signs of volcanic
activity everywhere in Iceland.
Lavafields, ash deserts,
fumaroles, extinct volcanic
craters, as well as dormant and
not-so-dormant volcanoes are
vivid reminders of the power of
nature. Hekla – Iceland's most
famous volcano – has regular
eruptions and those at Surtsey
and Heimaey made the world's
headlines.
The thermal activity beneath the
Earth's crust also reveals itself in
the form of pools of steaming,
sulphurous mud, hot springs,
geysers and steam vents. Such
is the abundance of these hot

Red-necked phalarope

springs that the vast majority of
Icelandic homes use the hot
water as a source of heating.

Thingvellir National Park.

The shores of Thingvallavatn –
Iceland's largest lake – were the
site of the country's first
parliament in AD930. The area is
now a national park and its
status protects both this historic
spot and the wildlife and
dramatic, volcanic scenery of
the surrounding area.
Thingvellir is 30 miles (50km)
east of Reykjavík and is on the
itinerary of most tours from the
capital.
Scan the lake with binoculars
and you should see great
northern divers swimming low
in the water. They nest in
isolated and undisturbed spots
and their primary source of food
is the lake's population of arctic
char. You are perhaps most
likely to notice this handsome
bird as it rolls over to preen its
belly feathers. At this time the
pure white underside is
revealed.

PEACE AND QUIET

Saxifrages come in a remarkable variety of forms; this one is saxifraga cotyledon

Around the margin of Thingvallavatn, the tundra vegetation and dwarf birch scrub are the haunt of nesting golden plovers, whimbrels and ptarmigans. All these species keep a wary eye open for the occasional gyr falcon, a herring gull-sized bird of prey. Continue your journey away from Reykjavik and you will come to Geysir, the site of the world famous Great Geysir. The birch woodland and heathy habitat which surrounds this tourist spot is good for a variety of birdlife. Near by are the falls of Gullfoss. In addition to the dramatic scenery, harlequin ducks are sometimes seen on quiet stretches of river and stream. These ducks are named after the males' markings – he has extraordinary white patterning on his head, breast, wings and back. These marks are set against a background colour of very dark blue, with reddish flanks. Altogether a bird to keep an eye open for!

Skaftafell National Park

Skaftafell contains perhaps the greatest variety of habitat and wildlife of any area in Iceland. The scenery is undeniably magnificent: three glaciers descend from the Vatnajökull – not only Iceland's but also Europe's largest ice-cap – icebergs float in serene lakes and visitors can gaze across vast sand plains and areas of glacial outwash. Tundra heath and birch woodland add to the variety and provide suitable habitats for nesting birds and over 200 species of flowering plants. The national park lies north of the coast road and can be reached by driving east from Reykjavík; it is a full day's journey from the capital. Several trails radiate from the Skaftafell car park. One, which winds around the hillside, passes through downy birch and rowan woodland. Among the birds you might see are Iceland wrens and redwings, the latter species generally showing little fear of passing trekkers. The undergrowth is rich in plant life: look for wood cranesbill, wild angelica, harebell and lady's bedstraw, which are all common. Wood sorrel – a rare and protected species in Iceland – also grows here.

Rivers and streams cut the flat, glacial outwash plains at the foot of the glaciers. Grass of Parnassus is abundant here at certain times of the year. Despite its name, this is not a grass, but a particularly delicate flowering plant. The flower, with five white petals, smells very faintly of honey. Keen-eyed visitors may spot a curious lichen, *Thamnolia vermicularis*, which grows on the bare gravel here and resembles nothing so much as a writhing mass of white worms!

Nearby at Skeidarársandur is an immense colony of skuas which nest on the flat sand plains. Around 3,000 pairs of great skuas breed here, making it probably the most important nesting site in the world for this bird, which looks like a large brown gull. They resent any intrusion into their territory and will 'dive-bomb' human intruders who stray too close to a nest or a youngster. Occasionally they swoop so close that they draw blood with their claws.

Birds of Mývatn

The River Laxá, at the southwestern corner of the lake, is a renowned haunt of harlequin ducks, which can be seen in the turbulent water from the road. On the lake itself, however, look for scaup, Barrow's goldeneyes – almost the entire Icelandic population is found here – mallards, teals, gadwalls, wigeons, tufted ducks, shovelers and several other species; 15 species of wildfowl regularly breed here.

Slavonian grebes breed in good numbers as do red-necked phalaropes. Numbers of the latter species are swollen in the late summer by juveniles and adults from elsewhere in northern Iceland. On a calm day, these delightful little waders, which swim buoyantly on the water, can be seen dotting the surface of Mývatn as far as the eye can see.

Lake Mývatn

Without doubt, Lake Mývatn is *the* place to visit for the birdwatcher. Nowhere else in Iceland can you find such a range of breeding species of wildfowl or such incredible numbers – over 100,000 birds may be present after the breeding season. Ornithological interest is not confined simply to wildfowl: waders, grebes and terns also breed here in abundance. Although the landscape surrounding Mývatn is comparatively featureless, there are some spectacular volcanic features in the area, nearby sulphur pools and craters being but two examples. Mývatn is reached by driving south from Akureyri. Virtually the whole of the shoreline can be explored by road.

'Mývatn' literally means 'midge-lake' in Icelandic, a name which appears only too appropriate when birdwatching on a calm day in July or August. Both midges and blackflies breed here in super-abundance.

Barrow's goldeneye

Slavonian grebe

Only the blackflies bite, but the distinction may seem almost irrelevant when the insects are at their peak: their sheer numbers clog the eyes, nose, mouth and ears of all who venture too near the shoreline. Happily, if you retreat 100 yards/metres or so away from the water, the insect numbers drop off dramatically.

The underlying reason for the abundance of both insect and bird life at Mývatn lies in the nutrient-rich waters which feed the lake. The shallow water – allowing warming and sunlight penetration – encourages a rich summer growth of blue-green algae, which in turn supports the midge and blackfly larvae. Many of the species of birds feed directly on the insects, although some, such as great northern divers and goosanders, eat the brown trout and arctic char which also cash in on the bonanza.

Visitors to Lake Mývatn generally travel to and from Akureyri. Fields outside the town are good for wild flowers including small white orchids, slender gentians, louseworts, eyebrights and many more species. If you have time, visit the Botanical Gardens (there is also a small botanical garden in Reykjavík). Most of Iceland's common species grow here, clearly labelled, as well as many of the more unusual plants. Visitors from northwest Europe will be amused to find stinging nettle lovingly grown as one of Iceland's rarities!

Jökulsárgljúfur National Park

This dramatic national park lies in northeast Iceland and protects the Jökulsárgljúfur canyon, the largest of its kind in the country. The canyon is as varied as it is spectacular: in places the cliffs are sheer and imposing, while elsewhere, the valley floor is broad and flat, cut by streams and rivers and carpeted with lush vegetation. Three waterfalls – Hafragilsfoss, Dettifoss and Selfoss – add to the attraction of the area. The park has an excellent cross-section of Iceland's tundra-loving plants and birds.

Malarrif Cliffs and Snæfellsnes Peninsula

The Malarrif cliffs lie on the southern side of the Snæfellsnes peninsula, to the north of Reykjavík. The coastal scenery is dramatic, but it is for the seabird colonies that many people visit the area.

The drive from Reykjavík is comparatively long, especially considering that the city is only about 60 miles (100km) away in a straight line. However, there are always things to look out for *en route*: Iceland poppies adorn the roadside in summer, and colonies of arctic terns breed near the road in a few places. Slavonian grebes, red-necked phalaropes and red-throated divers can be seen from the car where the road passes close to pools and lakes.

Beside the coastal road there is a car park at Malarrif and from here it is a short walk to the cliff edge. The cliffs themselves have been eroded and weathered over the millenia by wind, rain and sea. Rock pinnacles and stacks have formed, but the ledges are best suited for the nesting birds. The best vantage points for the seabird colonies may vary from year to year according to where the birds are nesting, so explore the area. Try to find a spot where you can look *along* the cliff in safety. Never try to look over the cliff edge: you may alarm the nesting birds and you will most certainly alarm your companions. The cliffs are extremely precipitous and the sparse vegetation is deceptively slippery. It goes without saying that you should never throw things over the cliff.

Once you have found a good vantage point you will see hundreds of guillemots lined up side-by-side along the ledges. Many of these birds will be the 'bridled' form – they look as though they are wearing white spectacles – which is increasingly common at northerly latitudes.

Look closely at each bird because their close relative, Brünnich's guillemot, also occurs here. This is a truly arctic species, not found in more southerly seabird colonies, and

Malarrif must be one of the easiest and most reliable places in Europe to see this species. It is superficially similar to the common guillemot; it is roughly the same size but has a stouter bill – the guillemot's is more slender and tapering – and a prominent white stripe along the cutting edge of the lower mandible.

Further along the southern coast of the peninsula from Malarrif are excellent areas of tundra which are blanketed in mosses and lichens. Birds such as ptarmigan, redwings, snow buntings and meadow pipits are common, while along turbulent streams, fringed with carpets of cotton grass, harlequin ducks

The seabird cliffs at Malarrif

PEACE AND QUIET

Black guillemot

can be found. Along the coast, for example near the fishing community at Arnastapi, look for eider ducks: they often nest near the shore and, when the young have hatched, form 'creches' with several adults looking after 20 or 30 ducklings. Along the northern coast of the Snæfellsnes peninsula, colonies of arctic terns and glaucous gulls can be found, often beside the road. There is also a reasonable chance of seeing gyr falcons and white-tailed eagles. Both species are sensitive to disturbance and completely protected by Icelandic law and so must never, under any circumstances, be approached near the nest. The port of Stykkishólmur gives access to the huge bay of Breiðafjördur, dotted with small islands which are extremely

important for nesting seabirds. Of these, Flatey is among the most important and is certainly the most frequently visited. The whole Breiðafjördur area, and Flatey in particular, is good for eiders, puffins, great black-backed gulls, snow buntings, white wagtails, redshanks and snipe, each nesting in appropriate habitats. One of the most endearing nesting birds here is the black guillemot, resplendent in black plumage, white wing panels and bright orange-red feet and gape (opened mouth). They often nest under boulders and off-duty birds sit around seemingly 'chatting' to each other.

The North Coast
Continuing along the road from Snæfellsnes towards Akureyri, the perimeter roads pass by some enchanting coastline: fiord valleys, green-turfed cliffs and lichen-covered lavafields run down to the sea. For those who drive this far, this is one of the most attractive and unspoilt stretches of accessible Iceland. As with most Icelandic roads, those along the northern coast should be treated with considerable respect and driven at a slow speed. This not only allows you to see more wildlife but also increases the chances of survival for many of the birds.
Colonies of arctic terns can be found all along the coast, and unfortunately pay little attention to the presence of roads and vehicles. Recently fledged youngsters on the road are a frequent sight and the carnage

Plants of the tundra

Flowering plants to look out for
on tundra include:
   Small white orchid
   Boreal orchid
   Coralroot orchid
   Stone bramble
   Dwarf cornel
   Boreal fleabane
   Alpine bartsia
   Scottish asphodel
   Bearberry
   Highland cudweed
On rocky outcrops look for:
   Purple saxifrage
   Drooping saxifrage
   Yellow mountain saxifrage
   Moss campion
   Hairy stonecrop
   Alpine catchfly
   Sticky catchfly
   Rock speedwell

caused by traffic in some areas is disturbing.

Whenever a cliff-top view presents itself, stop and scan the sea below for birds. In the summer months, huge 'rafts' of eider ducks, many of them moulting males in rather inelegant plumage, gather in sheltered bays. Keen birdwatchers may wish to scrutinise these flocks in detail because king eiders are regular, if rather rare, breeders and visitors to this coast.

Farther Afield

The interior – while much of Iceland's perimeter is accessible to ordinary vehicles, the interior is an entirely different matter. Tracks and trails are only opened during the summer months and then only at the discretion of officials. Four-wheel drive vehicles are required and all provisions must be taken with you at the start –

there are no facilities. The rewards, however, more than repay the effort expended. Snowy owls breed here, and anyone who stays for more than a few days stands a good chance of seeing one of these spectacular birds. Gyr falcons and arctic foxes are also more regularly seen in the interior than around the perimeter.

The Westman Islands – these lie off the southwest coast within sight of Iceland's mainland. They contain some of the most important seabird colonies in Europe, let alone Iceland. The species include Manx shearwater, storm petrel and Leach's petrel, as well as more widespread species like puffin, guillemot, fulmar and kittiwake. Regrettably, puffin catching still continues, even though nowadays it can be categorised more a 'sport' than a necessity.

Puffins never fail to endear

PEACE AND QUIET

The island group contains Surtsey and Heimaey, both of which have hit the headlines: the former was created by eruptions between 1963 and 1967, while the latter had to be evacuated in 1973 due to life-threatening volcanic activity.

Hornstrandir Landscape Reserve – an isolated and dramatic region in northwest Iceland which can only be explored on foot or by boat. The seabird colonies, in particular, are outstanding.

Whaling

Iceland's coastal waters are among the richest feeding grounds in the North Atlantic and support an abundance of marine life. Among the inhabitants of this productive environment, whales are still regularly seen even though their populations have been dramatically reduced by whaling activities. Despite concerns expressed by the International Whaling Commission (of which Iceland is a member) about dangerously low populations, and a moratorium (due to expire soon) on commercial whaling, Iceland still continues to kill finback and sei whales for 'research'.

The scientific study of whales elsewhere in the world is largely confined to intense observational programmes and non-destructive means of sampling and monitoring. These methods form part of Iceland's programme but they also kill whales as part of their studies. A declared objective of this research is to assess under what circumstances commercial whaling can resume again.

To some, the scientific rationale behind these 'experiments' is rather dubious and cynics might be forgiven for interpreting it as a means of keeping a 'foot in the door' for commercial whaling; especially since most of the meat from these 'studies' is exported frozen to Japan and 'prepared' under Japanese supervision!

At a time when world opinion would appear to regard commercial whaling as an unnecessary act of ecological vandalism, Iceland is still resolved to exploit whales as a 'resource' and looks to the future restoration of this controversial industry.

Yet comparatively few people make a living from whaling in Iceland and none of the whale-meat consumers in Iceland or Japan depend upon it for their survival – it is a high-priced luxury commodity in Japan.

Moral arguments apart, where is the economic need for whaling, and are there any alternatives? It is interesting to contrast the situation in Iceland with that on the coast of New England in the US. Here whale-watching trips – to see living whales – are now worth millions of dollars annually; it is a big business with hundreds, if not thousands, of boats operating day trips to see the whales at close range. How much more profitable might it be for the Icelandic economy if it were to adopt this form of 'exploitation' of these extraordinary and beautiful creatures?

FOOD AND DRINK

Iceland's main dishes are based on fish and lamb, and with tourist numbers increasing, restaurants are constantly experimenting with new ways of preparing these staples to tempt our palates.

Many of the fish will be known to visitors, for example cod, salmon, trout and halibut, but others, like redfish, may not be so familiar. While visitors may be used to straightforward cuts like cod steaks, the Icelanders go in for delicacies like cod's cheeks – highly recommended! During the summer months, many sheep are grazed up in the uninhabited highlands and mountain lamb is highly prized. Some of the better-known dishes that are 'peculiar' to Iceland are **hangikjöt** (smoked lamb), **skyr** (soft cheese made from curdled milk), **hardfiskur** (wind-dried fish), **svid** (singed sheep's head) and **hákarl** (cured shark meat).

The main vegetable is the potato, but cabbages, onions and many other vegetables in use in northern Europe are also common. There can be a lack of variety in the home-grown ingredients and this stems from the shortness of the growing season and the lack of good agricultural land. However, the increasing use of geothermal energy to heat greenhouses has resulted in the regular appearance of fresh tomatoes, cucumbers and other vegetables onto Icelandic tables.

Growing tourist influence in Iceland has had its effects on the culinary arts; some, like the opening of numerous pizza restaurants in Reykjavík and the selling of hot dogs in the roadside cafés, will be all too familiar to visitors as 'international cuisine'.

Fishermen, Reykjavík harbour

Fish cured the Icelandic way

In general, most of the restaurants in the towns and settlements (that is, excluding Reykjavík) are in the hotels, so that is the first port of call when looking for a place to eat. Many restaurants have their own specialities, so it is best to ask a waiter what is in a particular dish if you are uncertain; the waiters and waitresses are invariably very knowledgeable and helpful. Portions are usually generous, so some visitors might be quite satisfied with just one course for a meal.

It has to be said that eating in Iceland is not cheap. Meals may cost twice or more what you might expect to pay at home. There are no cheap pub meals either, but a number of hotels and restaurants have a 'Sumarréttir' ('Tourist Menu') scheme whereby a limited choice of food is offered at a much-reduced price. Look out for 'Tourist Menu' stickers on doors and windows. Many roadside cafés offer full meals and these are generally good and rather cheaper than in restaurants; in general, visitors will probably find these places more convenient when they are travelling because of their roadside location, faster service and longer opening hours. Alcohol is very expensive and visitors may wish to take in their duty-free allowance, purchasing it either at their home airport or at Keflavík airport, which has a duty-free shop for *incoming* passengers. Many hotels and restaurants have bars and Reykjavík has a number of pubs, but these can be exceptionally busy at weekends. Alcohol can only be bought at the State Monopoly Shops which are found in a number of settlements around the country; there is one in Reykjavík's Kringlan shopping mall. It was only in 1989 that strong beer was freely allowed in Iceland; before that only a rather weak variety was available. However, most common 'international' drinks are sold and Icelanders are adopting the habit of drinking wine with restaurant meals.

SHOPPING

For a variety of reasons (cost of transport, the size of the market etc), goods in Iceland tend to be rather expensive. It pays to shop around and if you are travelling around the country it is advisable to consider buying presents in a large supermarket in the countryside rather than paying extra in the capital's tourist shops.

The most popular things to take home are the excellent woollen goods which are on sale everywhere in Iceland, but have a good look round first as prices and quality vary. Most of them have been expertly machine-knitted, but some are knitted by hand. Reykjavík has numerous shops selling such goods and these are wonderful for browsing in. A number of these shops sell wool and (English-language) patterns and you may find these of interest if you want to knit your own garments. The best bargains are probably found in the woollen mills' factory shops so keep a lookout for them.

There are many small potteries in Iceland and many examples of their work are on sale in the gift shops and even in some of the larger supermarkets. 'Lava ware', with bits of lava incorporated into the pottery, is distinctive.

Visitors leaving the country via Keflavík airport will find a large Icemart shop in the departure lounge selling books, woollens, vacuum-packed fish, cheeses and other goods.

Shopping for food needs care as prices are high compared to other countries. Food quality is best in the larger settlements and the prices tend to be cheaper there also. Super-markets are generally the best bet. Take the opportunity to visit farms with glasshouses if they are selling their produce as there are often very good bargains in such places. Bread is usually excellent and a wide variety of cheeses is produced. Salmon and prawns may be good buys.

The 'What to See' section mentions the main places in each region where shopping

Woollen goods on sale in Reykjavík

facilities are to be found.
However, be warned that shops
can be far apart – just look at a
map of Iceland to see the
distances between the
settlements! – so it is sensible to
keep a stock of food and to shop
whenever the opportunity
arises. Generally, all the
settlements will have a
supermarket where food,
toiletries, batteries, vacuum
flasks and other such tourist
necessities can be purchased.
Some of the settlements have
particularly good supermarkets
(which stock clothes, camping
equipment etc) and these are
mentioned where they are in
places that are of 'strategic
importance', meaning, it's a long
way to the next one! Many
roadside cafés have small
supermarkets and these are
invaluable.
Visitors will find that the
settlements' supermarkets
cannot afford to keep a wide
range of goods. The size of
surrounding population does not
warrant that. Instead, many
Icelanders go to Akureyri or
Reykjavík to do their shopping
or shop by mail order. In
comparison to the settlements,
almost anything is available in
Reykjavík and visitors will
recognise familiar
internationally-known brands of
vehicles, clothes, washing
machines etc. Indeed, when you
browse around the capital's
shops you will soon see just how
gadget-conscious the
Icelanders are, especially when
it comes to consumer durables
and items like car phones.
Many goods are subject to a
24½ per cent Value Added Tax

but this can be refunded to
visitors in some circumstances.
To qualify for a refund the
goods must cost over a certain
amount (currently Ikr5,000), they
must leave the country within 30
days of purchase and a special
refund voucher must be made
out at the time of purchase (this
needs your passport number).
The goods must then be packed
in sealed bags and be
unopened when taken through
Customs. If flying, the bags must
be taken on board as hand
luggage unless they are
woollens. When in Keflavík
airport, the voucher should be
presented at the duty-free shop
where a cash refund will be
made. Visitors leaving from
Seydisfjördur should see the
Customs Officers there and ask
them to sign the voucher which
you then send to the duty-free
shop at Keflavík airport and wait
for the money to be sent to you.
Note that not all the VAT is
refunded.

ACCOMMODATION

There are various different
types of accommodation
available in Iceland and the
comments here exclude
consideration of the capital,
which is dealt with on its own in
the 'What to See' section.
Almost all the settlements have
a hotel; these establishments
vary in size, facilities and price
and many are open throughout
the year. Most settlements will
also have guesthouses which
are basically small hotels that
can accommodate a few people;
their size and facilities are, of
course, less than those of the

Reykjavík's Hotel Borg

hotels and they are not always open throughout the year. Some private houses also take guests, but this type of accommodation is generally only available during the summer.

There is only one national chain of hotels, the Edda Hotels. These are dual-purpose buildings as they are home to schoolchildren during term-time and are then turned into tourist hotels for the three months of the school holidays. They can sometimes be rather institutional in character, but they are clean and warm and often have a heated swimming pool. These hotels are found in some towns and also in the countryside. They are managed during the summer by the Iceland Tourist Bureau and an 'Open Edda Voucher' is available at a discounted price which can then be used in the 16 Edda Hotels and in a number of other places, giving a total of some 40 participating establishments (some of which are in Reykjavík).

There is an Icelandic Youth Hostels Association and there are about 16 hostels, dotted fairly evenly around the country. They range from small buildings that take only 12 or so guests to much larger places that are more like small hotels. Perhaps the most interesting places to stay at are the farmhouses and there is now a network of around 100 farms that take in visitors. Many of these are far away from settlements and consequently remote from other types of accommodation. These are marketed through Farm Holidays in Iceland, Bændahollin, Hagatorg, Reykjavík, and their brochure is full of ideas worth considering. The farmers will be able to suggest walking routes in their area; they might also have ponies for hire and be able to arrange fishing in the local rivers.

Visitors who are travelling

through the interior will find tourist huts at a number of the best known stopping points but these can be very busy and may be fully booked. They are owned by clubs whose parties take priority.

One feature that may be of interest to visitors on a tight budget is that many establishments, including some hotels, offer sleeping bag accommodation; this is known as *svefnpokapláss*.

Each of the areas described in the 'What to See' section has information about a selection of places at which to stay, but visitors to Iceland who are arranging their own itinerary do not generally make the choice of hotel a high priority. Indeed, it is the other way round – they plan what places they want to visit and then find out what accommodation is available.

CULTURE, ENTERTAINMENT AND NIGHTLIFE

The definition of 'culture' is very wide and each country's expression of its own culture depends on a multitude of factors like its history, its physical environment and the personality of its people. Iceland's great cultural achievement, and one which is highly regarded around the world, is the Sagas, the tales of the Norsemen and their exploits.

Many of the main strands of Icelandic 'culture' are rooted in the spoken and printed word. The Sagas were first told as tales at gatherings like the annual Althing well before they were written down. The later manuscripts (and the religious

Look out for street theatre

books that were also produced) were sometimes illuminated with beautiful designs. Visitors should take the opportunity to read some of the Sagas, perhaps *Njals Saga* or *Egils Saga*. Scots visitors may find something of interest in *Orkneyinga Saga*, while visitors from North America can learn about the exploration of their own continent in the *Vinland Sagas*.

The last 200 years have maintained but diversified this interest in literature. Today, the importance of the written word is emphasised by the fact that a population of only a quarter of a million, using a language that no other nation uses, produces six daily newspapers and publishes 1,000 books a year. This is an astonishing achievement and reflects the fact that culture is not the preserve of an élite, but the property of the nation as a whole. The country can also boast one of the world's highest rates of literacy and its students regularly (through necessity) use foreign-language textbooks. The grinding poverty of earlier centuries, the paucity of good building materials, the lack of private or public wealth, the 'isolation' of the language and the smallness of the population have meant that there is no long tradition of great architecture, sculpture or painting. The long winter nights, however, gave Icelanders time for talking, reading, writing and for handicrafts like embroidery and woodworking. Today, the visual arts have become very important and visitors will notice the number of sculptures gracing

parks and open areas in the settlements. Painting has also been taken up enthusiastically, and art galleries in Reykjavík and in other places will have much to interest art-minded visitors.

When touring round the country, the main historical 'sites' are not battlefields, castles, mansions or lavishly-decorated museums but small folk museums that preserve the handiwork of past generations, and the small timber and turf farmhouses and churches that show the style of buildings of bygone days. The 'What to See' section mentions a number of these museums, farms and churches.

Many forms of artistic expression such as choir singing, instrumental concerts and the performance of plays could only really develop late in Iceland's history when the city of Reykjavík grew and had enough people to take part in and support these activities. Today, Reykjavík is the artistic centre of organised cultural activities, though groups of artistes make tours of the settlements at various times of the year. Reykjavík's biennial Arts Festival is held in the summer and it offers ballet, plays, concerts, art exhibitions and a host of other forms of entertainment.

News from Iceland (see **Directory**) is normally a very good source of information for what is happening in the arts world and local Tourist Information Centres should have information about forthcoming events.

WEATHER AND WHEN TO GO

The main factors affecting the Icelandic weather are the country's location, the warm and wet air currents from the southwest, the cold air coming from the Arctic and the local effects of the ice-caps, especially the massive Vatnajökull.

The Gulf Stream brings warm and damp air to southwestern and southern Iceland and this results in a fairly high rainfall over the year. Rainy weather can last for a few days at a time, even in the middle of the summer. Once you see the greenness of the grass and the lushness of the mosses on the lavafields, you will get an idea of how wet the region can be at times. Once these winds move farther northeastwards they lose much of their moisture, especially to the ice-caps, making the north and northeast much drier than the rest of the country as they are in the ice-caps' 'rain shadow'.

However, the north takes the brunt of the cold Arctic winds and these can be really chilling in exposed areas and can make the weather somewhat 'bracing' – but much drier, and that is why many visitors like to get to this part of the country.

July and August are the peak tourist months and most of the interior routes should be open for much of this two-month period. In addition, hotels, museums, pony trekking, bus trips and other activities of interest should all be available then. These are generally the warmest months and it can be warm (20°C/70°F or more) in sheltered areas, so sunbathing is a real possibility! Having said that, visitors should expect some days when there is low cloud and some rain.

May and June are generally drier than these peak months but the tours and trips may not have started as there are fewer visitors, the temperatures are lower and there will still be

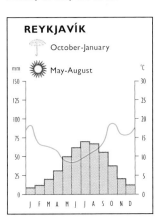

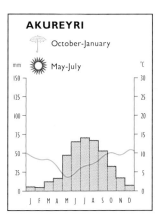

Skiddooing on Skálafellsjökull

quite a bit of snow about. In addition, some interior tracks might not open until July. Iceland is of course the land of the midnight sun and visitors will soon find that they lose track of time in June and July as it never really gets dark; midnight walks are quite the norm. Once August comes, the nights are getting rather longer and evening walks are usually curtailed about 22.00hrs or so. The Icelandic tourist industry is endeavouring to extend its tourist season and is welcoming increasing numbers of visitors on 'short breaks' outside the normal tourist season. This type of holiday usually involves staying in Reykjavík and going on day trips to places like Thingvellir, Geysir (and Strokkur), Gullfoss, the Blue Lagoon and Heimaey. Winter sports enthusiasts may consider a winter holiday in Iceland and skiing and skiddooing are popular, but the weather can be extremely unpredictable at this time of year and there are few hours of daylight.

The best way of summing up the weather is with the famous Icelandic saying 'If you do not like the weather, then just wait a minute and it will change'! For this reason, visitors need to be prepared for all sorts of weather, unless you are going to stay in a bus or hotel all the time. Since almost everyone is going to do some walking and as you will find out quite quickly that there are few trees to shelter under when it rains, you should look at the items of clothing mentioned in the **Walking** part of the Directory. In addition to waterproof walking clothes, an umbrella is a very handy item. Inadequate clothing not only ruins your holiday, in Iceland's extreme climate it can also be dangerous.

Looking into the glacial abyss at Skálafellsjökull

HOW TO BE A LOCAL

It is sometimes said that it is difficult to get to know the Icelanders, but visitors will soon find that they are made welcome guests in their country. You will probably be addressed by your first name, even in banks and other business premises, and you should answer using the person's first name if you know it.

Icelanders often seem to belong to one huge extended family. When two Icelanders meet for the first time, there is a very good chance that they will have an acquaintance or two in common and they will soon be chatting away like long-lost pals. Icelanders' names are in the form of patronymics, with family names rather uncommon. When a couple marry they often keep their own individual names and the children take their last names from the father's first name. In the case of the father being called Hannes Sveinsson, his son might be called Gunnar Hannesson and the daughter might be called Gudrún Hannesdóttir. This results in all four members of this family (parents and children) all having different second names. Rather confusing for non-Icelanders.

Icelanders generally have a great knowledge of their own country and are usually well-versed in its history, literature and landscape. They regard their country as full of surprises (and it is!) and are always keen to tell enquirers about the history of a particular place or some old tale connected with it. Visitors will soon find that the possession of a modicum of knowledge about the country is the best way of tapping even more information from an Icelander keen to extol the beauty of the country. The Icelanders' great love of the countryside is shown by the numbers of families who go camping during the summer weekends, but while visitors tend to stay in the campsites near the major attractions, many Icelandic families are attracted to the quiet wooded areas where they can get away from the pressure of Reykjavík life and enjoy the peace and quiet that is so readily available in the countryside. If you come across any of these unofficial campsites then you will probably have come across a veritable haven. Summer homes are also popular with the Icelanders. Some of these might be purpose-built wooden chalets, while older buildings might be an old family home that is used only in summer now that economic circumstances have drawn people to Reykjavík.

There are a few pubs outside the capital and at weekends the Icelanders might be out in the countryside or visiting friends and relatives. For many Icelanders, however, it is very difficult to get away from their work in the summer, usually because they might have two, three or even more jobs. Once the summer weather comes, farmwork starts in earnest, the construction industry picks up, the tourist industry comes alive and a host of part-time summer jobs suddenly need to be filled. Students and teachers often take up jobs in the tourist industry and children are soon given work to do as well. Only a generation or so ago, huge numbers of children used to spend their summer holidays working on the farms, helping with the animals and doing small jobs around the place. There is now much less of this and instead many of the children in the towns spend part of the long school holidays doing community work such as keeping parks tidy or painting walls. There are usually never enough people about to do all the work during the busy but brief months of summer.

Since many young people watch English-language television programmes and as most students have to work with foreign-language textbooks, visitors will soon find that there are few language barriers, at least with young people and people employed in the tourist industry. Faced with this, it is all too easy not to attempt to use Icelandic, and although the language is very complex, an honest attempt to use a few words of Icelandic is always appreciated.

CHILDREN

Parents will have to consider very carefully the pros and cons of taking children to Iceland. It is not really the kind of holiday destination for young children if they have been brought up on beach holidays or taken to places where sunshine is virtually guaranteed. However, for older children, there could hardly be a more exciting place to spend a summer holiday – but only if the child is keen on outdoor activities.

Apart from seeing geysers, bubbling mudpools and icebergs, children might find great enjoyment in walking, horse riding, looking at seabirds

One in four Icelanders are children

and visiting the outdoor swimming pools.

One important attraction might be the opportunity of staying in farmhouse accommodation. Apart from being a cheaper type of accommodation than a hotel – an important factor in a family holiday – there is often the chance to work with the farm animals, help bring in the hay or do other chores about the farm. [It is quite possible that other children (or grandchildren of the farmer) might also be there.] In addition, farmers might be able to arrange horse riding or fishing in a local lake or river.

TIGHT BUDGET

A holiday in Iceland is certainly not going to be cheap, particularly with food being very expensive, but there are ways of keeping costs down. Further help on budgeting should be sought from a tour operator as package deals with the air fare combined with internal flights, a bus pass or youth hostel vouchers might be available. Perhaps surprisingly, these can work out not much more expensive than taking the ferries from the UK to Iceland (via the Faeroes).

Once in Iceland, buses are not expensive though you will have to decide whether it is worth getting the Omnibus Passport or the Full-Circle Passport tickets. There is not a great deal of long distance traffic in Iceland (excepting visitors, of course) so hitch-hiking can be unreliable, especially in areas of low population. Cycling is another

viable form of transport, but again you should be prepared to be flexible and consider taking the bus when necessary. One journey to be considered carefully is the section of the ring road between Egilsstadir and Mývatn. This is across a barren windswept desert where summer snowstorms are not uncommon. Consider taking the scheduled bus.

● Camping is certainly the cheapest form of accommodation, but cyclists and walkers may not wish to carry a tent with them. The budget alternatives are places that offer sleeping bag accommodation, youth hostels and farmhouse accommodation. However, in places that offer sleeping bag accommodation, there may not be a kitchen available for cooking your own meals.

● In Reykjavik, the cheapest places to stay are the youth hostels and with families offering 'bed and breakfast' accommodation.

● Food is expensive, so it is best to make your purchases in the larger supermarkets.

● When buying meals, the roadside cafés and cafeterias in the towns are probably the best places to go.

SPECIAL EVENTS

Since the country's population is so small and widely scattered (outside Reykjavik that is), there are few special events during the summer months. The most important ones are Reykjavik's Arts Festival (June, biennial), Reykjavík's marathon (August) and the National Horse

Championship (July). This major equestrian event takes place every four years (at different locations) and lasts about a week, but there is always a national event of some description each summer. There are also a number of events that have special significance in the history and folklore of the land. The start of the fourth month of winter (Thorri) is celebrated with a Thorrablot, held on the Friday in the 13th week of winter (19–25 January). Once the long and dark days of winter are over, the First Day of Summer is welcomed on the Thursday in the period April 19–25 – no matter what that day's weather is like! 17 June is National Day, the date celebrating the birthday of Jón Sigurdsson and the declaration of the Icelandic Republic in 1944.

Celebrating National Day

SPORT

As befits an island nation, and especially one whose main industry is fishing, Icelanders are keen swimmers. The country's weather certainly does not encourage seabathing, but most settlements have swimming pools heated by natural hot water. These are superb places to relax in and you should definitely try to visit some of them. There are usually small 'hot pots' beside the main pool and these can be very hot. Reykjavík's main pool has a temperature of 28/29°C (80°F) and its hot pots' temperatures vary from 35°C (95°F) up to 45°C (105°F)! You must shower without a costume before you enter any of the pools.

Football is a popular sport and many settlements have pitches. The major teams regularly play against each other but a number of the top players seek full-time professional jobs with football clubs overseas.

Golf is increasing in popularity and there are over 20 courses, ranging from six to 18 holes. Most of the main towns have a course and the 18-hole courses are found in Reykjavík, Akureyri, Hella (on the south coast), Gardur and Hafnarfjördur (both on the northern coast of Reykjanes peninsula) and Ólafsvik (on the northern coast of Snæfellsnes peninsula). The Akureyri Golf Club has an annual 36-hole

SPORT

competition called 'The Arctic Open' which starts just before midnight and is played through the night!

The weather dictates that many sports can only be played indoors and handball and badminton are among the popular sports now that special halls have been built. The Icelandic handball team is now regarded as being world-class, a wonderful accolade for a small nation that is so keen on participatory sport. One long-established sport peculiar to Iceland is **glíma**, a form of wrestling; interestingly, boxing is illegal.

The first Viking settlers brought horses with them and their sturdy sure-footedness was invaluable in crossing deserts, rivers and lavafields. Horses are still used by farmers when they are on the autumn round-up of sheep in the highlands, but horse riding is now more of a pastime than a necessity. However, it is an increasingly popular activity with visitors and rides varying from a couple of hours to a few days are available from many farms. The main riding districts are in the southwest, the west and the north (especially around Skagafjördur), but horses will be seen in most parts of the country.

Skiing is popular and there are ski tows near a number of towns including Reykjavík, Akureyri, Egilsstadir and Ísafjördur. However, the weather can be rather unpredictable during the season. Summer skiing is available on the Kerlingarfjöll mountains which are between the ice-caps of Langjökull and Hofsjökull, but this area can only be reached by a four-wheel drive vehicle.

Fishing, especially for salmon and trout, is popular with many Icelanders and fishing holidays are available, though the salmon rivers can be very expensive.

Thermal swimming pools are popular

DIRECTORY

Contents

Arriving

By air

Icelandair is the country's national carrier and there are regular scheduled flights from many European and American cities to Iceland. There are flights from Glasgow, London, New York, Orlando and Baltimore/Washington and these all land at the **Leifur Eiríksson Terminal** which is at Keflavík on Reykjanes peninsula just 30 miles (48km) southwest of Reykjavik. The airport, opened in 1987, has the unusual distinction of possessing a duty-free shop for *incoming* passengers! A good bus service connects the airport to Icelandair's Reykjavik terminal which is at the Hotel Loftleidir. Lufthansa and SAS have a small number of flights to Keflavík from Frankfurt and Copenhagen respectively, and there is also an Icelandair service between the Faeroes and Egilsstadir, which is in the Eastern Fiords. Airport taxes are normally included in the cost of your holiday – but check.

Icelandair

As the national carrier, Icelandair has offices in many countries. In some countries, Icelandair operates as a tour operator while in others they are prevented by law; in those latter countries (such as the UK) they can supply the names and addresses of tour operators.
Major Icelandair offices include:
Room 248, Terminal Building, Glasgow Airport, Paisley PA3 2TD, UK.
172 Tottenham Court Road, London WP1 9LG, UK.
610B Fifth Avenue, Rockefeller Center, New York, NY 10020, US.
Orlando (US): toll-free number at Orlando International Airport: 1-800-223-5500.

By sea

Iceland is served by two ferry companies, the Smyril Line which sails between the Faeroe Islands and Seydisfjördur in the Eastern Fiords and Eimskip which connects a number of European ports with Reykjavik. The Faeroese Smyril Line operates a popular summer-only service between Tórshavn in the Faeroes and Seydisfjördur and these are but two of the ports that the large and comfortable *Norröna* plies between. The ship's week-long route is:

Tórshavn – Hanstholm (Denmark) – Tórshavn – Lerwick (Shetland) – Bergen (Norway) – Lerwick – Tórshavn – Seydisfjördur – Tórshavn. This complicated journey means that UK visitors must first get to Shetland, the most convenient way being by the P & O ferry from Aberdeen. In addition, the week-long timetable entails visitors having an enforced stop-over on the return journey in the Faeroes while the ship sails to other European ports. However, the Faeroes are a fascinating group of islands that are well worth exploring. The Eimskip service is essentially utilising spare passenger space on a roll-on/roll-off container ship. While this might sound a little spartan, especially for crossing the North Atlantic, you can always while away the time relaxing in the ship's swimming pool! The Eimskip service operates throughout the year and connects Reykjavík with the ports of Immingham (England), Hamburg (Germany), Antwerp (Belgium) and Rotterdam (Netherlands). It may be of use to some visitors to note that unaccompanied vehicles can be sent to Reykjavík on the Eimskip freighters; this can be useful if you cannot spare the time for the sea journey and decide to fly.

Passports and visas

Visitors need a passport unless they are Nordic nationals arriving from a Nordic country; visas are not required by those holding passports from the EC countries, Australia, the United States, Canada and many other countries; it is best to check with your tour operator if you think you may need a visa. In theory, you may be asked to show that you have a return ticket and enough funds for your visit.

Maps of Iceland

Maps of Iceland are drawn and published by the Icelandic Geodetic Survey which trades as Landmælingar Íslands on Laugavegur 178, Reykjavík. The most useful map for visitors is the one at 1:500,000 which is available either folded or in a handy spiral format. This map gives all the roads and settlements plus a mass of detail showing garages, huts and petrol stations. It also designates routes as either roads (with or without asphalt) or tracks and thus gives a good indication of the types of surfaces liable to be encountered. This map is highly recommended. Maps at 1:1,000,000 and 1:750,000 give the topography of the country and a geological map at 1:500,000 is also available.

A series of nine 'general maps' cover the country at 1:250,000 scale; these are very useful if you want a lot of detail. The beauty of these maps is that every farm is indicated and named and since all farms display their names at their gates, these maps allow you to know exactly where you are while travelling along the roads. More detailed maps are available for areas such as Mývatn, Skaftafell, Thingvellir and Hornstrandir.

Miscellaneous information

Free maps of Iceland, as well as individual ones of Reykjavik, Akureyri and a number of other settlements are available.

The small free handbook *Around Iceland* is a goldmine of information about all the settlements.

The monthly English-language newspaper *News from Iceland*, which is published by Iceland Review in Reykjavík, contains a wealth of information including background reports on such diverse matters as the fishing industry, the arts and the economy. Small maps of the national parks and similar areas are available from their campsites. Finally, there are vast numbers of free leaflets available, especially in Reykjavík, so obtain these as

soon as you land in the country. The Tourist Information Centre in Reykjavik (see page 121) is the best source of free booklets and maps.

Camping

The overwhelming majority of visitors to Iceland are attracted by the spectacular scenery and the outdoor life. Staying at campsites is certainly one of the best ways of seeing and appreciating this unique country.

There are campsites in almost every settlement, in the national parks and in most other areas accessible to visitors. Even for those who travel into the interior, there are campsites at the tourist huts. The Iceland Tourist Board publishes information on the most important sites around the country though their list is certainly not exhaustive. Many farms offering farmhouse accommodation also cater for campers. In addition, it is often possible to camp in places other than campsites (though not on cultivated land) but it is only courtesy to check with the

The campsite in Skaftafell: one of Iceland's many options

nearest farm when camping near farm land.

The campsites vary greatly in size and facilities. Reykjavík's is very well appointed and it even has a laundry and a covered cooking area; Skaftafell is another high-grade site which is very popular. While some of the sites are fairly quiet, some of them can be very busy (especially at holiday weekends!). Mývatn is usually busy and even some sites in the interior, like Hveravellir and Landmannalaugar, can become overcrowded. Unfortunately, this means that it can be a bit difficult to 'get away from it all'. In general, the best facilities are found on the sites in the bigger settlements, those close to the ring road or in settlements where there is a local source of geothermal energy (as there will probably be a swimming pool nearby).

Since the weather can be somewhat unpredictable, it is essential to take a sturdy and reliable tent. A good ridge tent is probably the best type. A warm sleeping bag is also needed as is a closed-cell mat or airbed. The coldest campsites are generally those in north-facing fiords, those at a high altitude (for example, in the interior) and those near glaciers.

Camping gas is widely available and canisters can be bought at roadside shops. The water is safe to drink everywhere as it will be free from pollution, but streams coming down from glaciers carry a tremendous amount of debris in them and this may lead to upset stomachs.

Chemist (see **Pharmacist**)

Crime

The level of crime in Iceland is extremely low. Law-breaking can usually be related to an over-indulgence in alcohol. Although the chances of being the victim of a personal attack or theft are minimal, visitors should take the normal precautions with passports, money, credit cards and cameras.

There are far fewer drug-related problems in Iceland than in other European countries and the authorities intend to keep it that way, so the penalties of importing drugs are high.

Customs Regulations

Visitors can take the following items into the country tax and duty-free: one litre of wine or other drinks (up to 21 per cent alcohol) or six litres of imported beer or eight litres of Icelandic beer, plus one litre of liquor up to 47 per cent alcohol, plus 200 cigarettes or the equivalent of other tobacco products. Icelandic currency up to Ikr14,000 can be taken in, but there is no limit to the amount of other currencies.

Visitors are allowed to take food into the country up to a limit of 22lbs (10kg) per person, but the following types of food are forbidden: uncooked meat and meat products, eggs, poultry products, butter and milk. Icelanders jealously guard their rivers and farms against infection brought in from abroad, so fishing equipment and horse-riding equipment must be disinfected at Customs unless you have obtained a certificate of disinfection from a veterinary surgeon or if the equipment is brand new.

Cycling

Every year, increasing numbers of cyclists go to Iceland and find touring the country a wonderfully exciting experience; it is, however, for fit and experienced cyclists only. A mountain bike is essential as its sturdy frame can cope with the rough road conditions. Icelandair will carry bicycles on their scheduled flights. The scheduled buses can also carry bicycles so cyclists need not commit themselves to long journeys when the weather is not promising. Indeed, it is worth considering cycling on the asphalt roads and using buses for many sections of the gravel roads; the 1:500,000 map will help in planning this. Cyclists obviously have to travel light and it should be possible to use farmhouse accommodation for most nights, so no tent need be carried.

Disabled People

Very few hotels have the proper facilities for catering for disabled people such as ramps, lifts and large bathrooms that will take wheelchairs, and it is essential to discuss the potential difficulties with your tour operator before you travel. A number of hotels in Reykjavík do offer suitable facilities and there are also hotels in Akureyri, Húsavík and Höfn that can manage to help but all these hotels tend to be the more expensive ones.

For further information contact

Cycling along the Kjölur

the **Icelandic Association of the Disabled** (tel: (91) 12512/26700).

Driving

It has to be said that driving a vehicle around Iceland is an experience – to say the least! A vehicle gives you the freedom to go where you like (within reason, see below) and the opportunity to choose where and when you want to stop, but drivers will have to be well-prepared for an adventure! Although what follows may suggest that a touring holiday in Iceland is more of a trial than anything else, the author whole-heartedly recommends taking or hiring a car. Once you get used to the roads, the driving becomes great fun! Honest!

Road conditions

Road surfaces in Iceland are probably the most difficult in Europe. Most of the settlements have asphalt roads and some 60 per cent of the ring road has a permanent surface, but the rest generally have just a gravel surface which is often rutted or dotted with potholes or corrugations. The 'tracks' are rougher still.

High winds have been known to blow away sections of roads and torrential rain can play havoc with the surfaces. However, this is far less likely to happen during the summer season. Large scrapers regularly travel along the roads to smooth their surfaces.

Notwithstanding the points made above, any modern family car should be able to cope with the ring road and with the roads that lead to the places described in the 'What to See' part of this book – excluding the tracks in the interior or those to Thórsmörk, Hallmundarhraun and Laki.

The 1:500,000 map is a good indicator of whether a road is actually a road – or a track.

Driving in the interior

Driving through the interior (and most certainly into Thórsmörk!) is only for four-wheel drive vehicles and this category excludes four-wheel drive versions of family saloons. The interior is a dangerous wasteland of sand, quicksand, gravel, lavafields and powerful glacial rivers and it is not for the inexperienced driver.

Documents

Drivers taking their own vehicles will need their own national driving licence. An International Driving Permit is not needed if you hold a pink European licence or a United States licence. A motoring organisation membership card

(AA, RAC, etc) should be taken in order to take advantage of the services of the FÍB (see below). You will also need your vehicle's insurance papers and a Green Card (to cover Denmark as well if you are travelling via the Faeroes). Your travel insurance should cover the vehicle too. Visitors from the UK should note that the AA's Five Star Travel Insurance policy covers Iceland and the Faeroes, but they recommend the Five Star Plus. Finally, you should carry the vehicle's Registration Certificate and have the appropriate nationality sticker or plate on the rear of the vehicle.

Driving in Iceland

Drive on the right. The roads can get exceptionally dusty at times and you can often see a vehicle's plume of dust well before you get sight of the vehicle itself. Care should be taken when dust and stones are thrown up by cars. An Icelandic driver will often signal that he wants to overtake by sounding his horn or flashing his lights and when you are being overtaken, slow down to lessen the chances of the windscreen being struck by pebbles. Drive with lights on all the time, even in broad daylight. Seat belts must be worn by all persons in the vehicle, including the back where belts are fitted.

While it is only sensible not to drive anywhere after consuming alcohol, this is especially true in Iceland. The price of alcohol, together with the necessity for full concentration on tough driving conditions means that few drivers will want to drink anyway! You should be aware that penalties for drunk driving are high and the legal limit is low compared with other countries.

One particular place where care is needed is at a junction where there are no give-way signs. Give way to vehicles coming from the right.

Although there are only a quarter of a million Icelanders, there are over twice as many sheep, and drivers will be forgiven for thinking that most of them wander across the road in front of their vehicle; this is a very real problem, so slow down and sound the horn.

The speed limit in built-up areas is normally 31mph (50kph) and outside it is generally 50mph (80kph), but it can be 56mph (90kph) on asphalt roads. The limit for vehicles towing a trailer is 44mph (70kph).

If you are in Iceland during June or July then the hours of daylight are exceptionally long and there is no need for night driving. Since the midsummer nights are very bright, you need not get too concerned about arriving late at campsites (very often Icelanders will arrive at a site at 22.00hrs or 23.00hrs in the evening) so you should not feel the need to rush journeys.

Road signs

Road signs are generally the same as those found in other European countries, but one sign of vital importance is **blindhæd**. This means just what it sounds like: a blind summit. Although you drive on the right in Iceland, when going along a gravel road it is often more comfortable to drive along the middle, thus avoiding the line of looser gravel that runs along either side and along the middle of the road. The blind summit is often marked with a pole in the centre of the road, so keep to the right of this.

Road distances are given in kilometres and speed limits are given in kilometres per hour (1 kilometre is about five-eighths of a mile).

Daunting prospect – an interior track

Fuel

Diesel, leaded petrol (98 octane) and unleaded petrol (92 octane) are found all over the country. It is best to keep the tank fairly full as there might be a long distance between petrol stations on the route you are following. A spare fuel can should be carried and this should be kept full in case you run out of fuel. Petrol is expensive so ensure you have always got enough cash with you; this is important as petrol stations do not accept credit cards for fuel purchases. There is no LPG in the country. Petrol stations are generally open until about 20.00hrs, though some may stay open rather later. Drivers of diesel-engined vehicles should note that diesel fuel is much cheaper than petrol and that there is an entry tax levied on diesel-engined vehicles (though this is not very high).

All settlements have petrol stations and some will also be found at important road junctions. Many are run in conjunction with roadside cafés and these establishments usually offer snacks, meals, toilets, telephones and shopping facilities.

Looking after the vehicle

If you are taking your own vehicle with you then it must be thoroughly checked before you leave, and particular attention paid to the parts that will be affected by vibration, for example the springs and shock absorbers. Tyres must be in good condition, including the spare tyre. In addition, it is best to have a few simple spare parts (spark plugs, points, fan belt, bulbs etc) with you, together with a 'do it yourself' manual and a reasonable toolkit.

The most common problems encountered are punctures and the loosening of items such as the exhaust. Roof-racks can be very troublesome, especially if they are of the bolted rather than welded variety, so check yours for tightness once it is loaded and also at the end of each day. Check the tyres at least once every day.

Breakdowns and accidents

Once you have located the nearest garage by consulting the tourist literature or by flagging down a passing motorist, you will find that they are marvellously adept at managing to fix almost any vehicles – after all, a local garage might be called upon to mend anything from a bicycle to a large bus. If any spare parts are needed they might have to be sent for from Reykjavík, a

Hateigskirkja, Reykjavík

very time-consuming business. It cannot be over-emphasised that your vehicle must be thoroughly checked before you leave home.

In the event of an accident you should contact the local police as well as your insurance company. If the police are involved, you may have to make a statement which you might not need to sign. It might also be advisable to contact the FÍB if you are a motoring club member. If someone is seriously injured or if you are charged with an offence then you should contact your embassy or consulate at once.

The FÍB

Félag Íslenzkra Bifreidaegenda (the FÍB) is the Icelandic Motoring Club and it is a member of the AIT (L'Alliance Internationale de Tourisme). It is a very small organisation and does not operate road patrols; instead, it can assist you with getting help from a garage should that be necessary. Drivers should carry their own motoring club card for, at the very least, it can often get you a sizeable discount on a garage bill if you pay cash. The club's office is at Borgartún 33, Reykjavík (tel: (91) 29999).

Car rental

Many visitors want to drive in Iceland but do not want to subject their own vehicle to the rough road conditions. There are many car rental companies in Iceland, most of them in the capital. Icelandair has its own fleet of cars and there are firms with franchises from the large international firms, for example Hertz. Many different types of vehicles are available, from small saloons to long-wheelbase four-wheel drive vehicles and it is also possible to hire caravanettes, minibuses and buses. The minimum age for hiring is 20, but this might be higher depending on the type of vehicle. Do not forget to take your driving licence.

Since the tourist season is very short there is a large demand for car hire during the summer. It is essential to book a vehicle well in advance of arrival. Car hire is expensive.

The method of charging is generally calculated on a daily basis with a distance charge on top of that; ensure that you know exactly how this charge is calculated and check that the quoted figure includes Value Added Tax. When collecting the vehicle, check its general condition, the mileage clock (though remember this will be in kilometres!), the spare wheel and the tools and ask what you should do in the event of a breakdown or accident. It is advisable to pay an accident damage waiver to minimise any possible claims against you and in any case find out what the insurance covers you for. It is especially important to know whether you are covered when you are off the road.

Electricity

The electrical supply is at 220V and the plugs are the common two-pin continental type so you may wish to take an adaptor with any electrical equipment you have. The mains frequency is 50Hz.

Embassies and Consulates

Australia: No embassy here, so the embassy in Copenhagen deals with matters: Kristianagde 21, DK 2100, Copenhagen (tel: (31) 262244).
Canada: Sudurlandsbraut, 10, Reykjavík (tel: (91) 680820).
Ireland: Thverholt 17–21, Reykjavík (tel: (91) 26300).
UK: Embassy: Laufásvegur 49, Reykjavík (tel: (91) 15883/4). Consul: Glerárgata 28, Akureyri (tel: (96) 21165).
US: Laufásvegur 21, Reykjavík (tel: (91) 29100).

Emergency Telephone Numbers

The inside front cover of the telephone directory gives emergency telephone numbers (and area codes) for the fire brigade, police, ambulance and the nearest hospital for all the major settlements. Someone in a roadside café or hotel should be able to help you and it should be remembered that many Icelanders have mobile telephones in their vehicles, as do many buses.

In Reykjavík, the following numbers should be used:
Ambulance: (91) 11100
Fire: (91) 11100
Police: (91) 11166
Hospital casualty: (91) 696600
Medical help: (91) 696600 (weekdays from 08.00–17.00hrs); (91) 21230 (weekdays from 17.00–18.00hrs and weekends)
Pharmacist: look up 'Apótek' in the Yellow Pages section of the telephone directory (one of the larger pharmacists should be open outside working hours)

Entertainment Information

Not many visitors go to Iceland for the nightlife, but it is there all the same. English-language publications that give information on what's on include: *News from Iceland, What's on in Reykjavík* and *What's on in Akureyri.* Other places where information can be found include the Tourist Information Centres, campsites and hotels.

Hveragerdi's hot-house horticulture

Entry Formalities (See **Arriving**)

Health Regulations

Visitors should have adequate holiday insurance and be aware of the name and address of their insurance company's Icelandic agent. Insurance should cover sickness, repatriation, personal belongings and vehicle, etc as appropriate. Iceland has reciprocal health-care agreements with a number of countries should a visitor fall ill, but check this first with your tour operator. There are no requirements for vaccination certificates, unless you have recently been in a country where smallpox is common. Hospitals are of very good quality and since doctors and other medical and professional staff probably used English-language medical textbooks while they were students, there should be no language difficulties.

Holidays

The public holidays are: New Year's Day, Maundy Thursday, Good Friday, Easter Sunday and Monday, first day of summer (variable), Labour Day (1 May), Ascension Day, Whit Sunday and Monday, National Day (17 June), August Bank Holiday, Christmas Eve, Christmas Day, Boxing Day, New Year's Eve. Only two of these are during the summer: National Day and the Bank Holiday (the first Monday in August). Hotels and campsites can be crowded over these two holidays.

Lost Property

Contact the local police station if you lose anything valuable; in Reykjavík the main police station is at Hverfisgata 113. Contact your embassy/consulate if you lose your passport.

Media

Reykjavík has an astonishing total of five daily papers, all of them rather partisan in their politics. Foreign English-language newspapers are available, for example at Eymundsson of Austurstræti 18, but these can be expensive. The television stations often carry English-language programmes and their news bulletins have good coverage of international events, so you can keep track of what is happening in the world (albeit in Icelandic!).

On the radio, Channel One carries a news item in English at 07.30hrs during the summer months and if you really want to keep up with the rest of the world, a recorded news bulletin can be obtained on (91) 693690 throughout the day and night. The NATO base at Keflavík has its own (American) radio station and this can be picked up in the Reykjavík/Reykjanes area. When visitors are on the south coast they may be able to pick up the BBC stations.

Money Matters

The banking system in Iceland is very modern and should present few difficulties to visitors, with one or two exceptions. It is probably best to take a quantity of your own currency and obtain Icelandic currency by one or more of the methods outlined in this section.

Icelandic currency

The unit of currency is the Icelandic krónur (kr or Ikr) and it is divided into 100 aurar; the aurar are not often used as they are of little value. The denominations of the notes are: 100, 500, 1,000 and 5,000 krónur; those of the coins are: 5, 10 and 50 aurar and 1, 10 and 50 krónur.

The banks

The banks are Búnaðarbanki Íslands, Íslandsbanki and Landsbanki Íslands. Almost every settlement has a bank. Their opening hours are generally Monday to Friday 09.15–16.00hrs.

The following places have banks that are open outside these hours: Keflavík airport, daily 06.30–18.30hrs; Hotel Loftleidir, daily (except Sunday in winter) 08.15–16.00hrs and 17.00–19.15hrs; Reykjavík Tourist Information Centre, Monday to Friday 16.30–18.00hrs and on Saturday 09.00–13.00hrs, from June to August.

Visitors staying at hotels should be able to change money at the reception desk.

Currency exchange

It is probably not worth getting Icelandic currency in your own country before you leave as the exchange rate may be poor; visitors arriving at Keflavík can use the bank at the airport. If it is closed, the airport bus (to Reykjavík) will take all major currencies.

Visitors can use cheques to obtain cash as long as they are Eurocheques (or similar) and supported by a suitable cheque guarantee card. Travellers' cheques are useful as they are easily exchanged and can be replaced by the bank if lost or stolen. Credit cards (Visa and Eurocard/Access/Mastercard) can also be used to obtain cash but the rate of interest charged by your own bank may be high. You may be asked to show your passport when obtaining currency. Remember to keep your exchange receipts in case you are asked to show them when changing your krónur back into your own currency when leaving Iceland.

Credit cards

Major credit cards (Visa and Access/Eurocard/Mastercard) can be used for obtaining cash, buying goods in many shops, restaurants and hotels (especially those regularly dealing with tourists) and in supermarkets. However, they cannot be used to purchase petrol.

Tax

When paying for major items such as car hire or presents, ensure that the price you have been quoted includes Value Added Tax (VAT), as this may be reclaimed (see **Shopping**). At present it is levied at a rate of $24\frac{1}{2}$ per cent.

Opening Times

Current opening times of museums etc in Reykjavík and Akureyri have been included in the 'What to See' section but these can vary and should be checked with current tourist information. Winter openings vary greatly, so check beforehand. Summer opening times may last from mid-May or the start of June to the end of August or mid-September. Many Icelanders have two, three or even more jobs during the summer and if helping to look after a small country museum is one of them, then the museum cannot really have long opening hours. If you arrive at a small country museum or little church and find it shut then enquire at a nearby farm or roadside café as they might hold the keys to the building. Shops are generally open on Monday to Friday 09.00–18.00hrs; lunchtime is from 12.00–13.00hrs. Not all shops will be open on Saturday (especially in the afternoon) and on Friday it is advisable to ensure that you have enough food for the weekend. Offices are generally open from Monday to Friday 09.00–17.00hrs.

Personal Safety

Sunburn is not a common complaint in Iceland, but if you are going skiing or venturing onto a glacier or onto Vatnajökull on a snowcat or skiddoo you should wear sunglasses and put protective cream on your face.
The weather can be cold and wet at times during the summer, and chapped skin or cold sores can occur. Take plenty of skin moisturiser. Pack the sticking plasters, too.
A first aid kit is advisable, containing as many as possible of these items: scissors, sticking plaster, bandages, aspirin or paracetamol, sun tan cream, skin moisturiser, antiseptic, anti-histamine cream and lip salve.

Pharmacies

There are pharmacists in many settlements and they can be located by looking up 'Apótek' in the telephone directory. In a district where there is no pharmacy a doctor will act as the pharmacist. Everyday toiletry items can often be purchased at a supermarket or roadside café.
Pharmacists cannot supply all the medicines that might normally be available over the counter at home, so you may have to visit a doctor for a specific medicine. This, together with the distance between settlements, means that it is best to have a good first aid kit with you. Take an adequate supply of any prescription medicine you are taking.

Photography

The unique Icelandic scenery and the wonderful quality of light make a visit to Iceland a virtual paradise for photographers. Inevitably, most

Ófaerufoss waterfall, Eldgjá

DIRECTORY

visitors use up more film than they ever thought possible so make sure you have enough – especially since film is very expensive. There are few photographic shops outside Reykjavík and Akureyri, but supermarkets stock the commoner types of film (and not much else).

It is important to protect your equipment from dust as even a stroll across a desert area will produce enough airborne dust to play havoc with photographic equipment. Cameras should be stored in zipped-up camera cases or pouches; many types of Velcro-fastened pockets are not enough to keep the dust out. Visitors to Iceland in June or July will be able to take advantage of the exceptionally long days, but although the days are long, the low level of light available for photography in the evening means that a tripod is a useful asset – especially for photographing the midnight sun.

Bird photography needs a long lens – a 400mm lens with a 35mm camera. A motordrive is useful for bird photography, for pictures of Strokkur or bubbling mud pools – or even a volcanic eruption if you are lucky enough to see one!

Places of Worship

Lutheranism is the established religion and although you will see many churches around the country, few Icelanders seem to attend church services regularly. Sunday services normally start at 11.00 or 14.00hrs.

Reykjavík has a Roman Catholic church and various congregations of other denominations.

There are still a small number of pagans who are followers of Thór.

Police

There is only one uniformed police force and police stations (*Lögrelan*) are to be found in many settlements. The inside front cover of the telephone directory lists those settlements where there is a police station

Looking up to Herdubreid's table-top summit

and gives their telephone numbers. The address can then be looked up in the main body of the directory. The main police station in Reykjavík is at Hverfisgata 113 (tel: (91) 11166).

Post Office
Post offices are found in nearly all settlements and they often double as the telephone office. The offices are identified by the sign *Póstur og Sími* ('Post and Telephone'). [Many of the buildings sprout aerials from the roof.] Post offices are generally open Monday to Friday 08.30/09.00hrs–16.30/17.00hrs. The post office at the BSÍ bus station in Reykjavík is also open until 19.30hrs on weekdays and from 08.00–15.00hrs on Saturdays.
Stamps are available at post offices and in other places such as roadside cafés; note that there are different postal rates for letters and postcards.

Public Transport
Although most Icelanders own their own vehicles, there is a well-organised public transport system which can be of great benefit to the tourist.
During the winter, the buses and aeroplanes save many people from the difficult and very tiring task of moving around the country in the cold weather.
There are no railways in Iceland and coastal passenger shipping services are not worth enquiring about.

Buses
Scheduled bus services are co-ordinated by the BSÍ bus station in Reykjavík. The main

hubs from which buses operate are Reykjavík, Akureyri, Höfn and Egilsstadir. Buses travel between these centres and there are also services that radiate out from them. Services reach all the inhabited parts of the country, round the coastal roads and across the interior (the latter only during the summer).
In settlements, the bus stop is usually at a hotel or roadside café, but it is useful to know that buses can be flagged down between settlements, and you can generally ask the driver if you can be set down between settlements too.
If one bus is full then another bus is arranged to take the extra passengers.
Although buses can be taken to nearly all the usual tourist haunts, they are rather infrequent. There is only one bus each way per day on the Reykjavík–Akureyri route – and that is the country's most important bus link! The timetable is called the *Leidabók* and it runs from May to April; although in Icelandic, it is straightforward to understand. For planning purposes, ask your tour operator for the English-language summary of the *Leidabók* as it is available well before the start of the tourist season.
There is an Omnibus Passport ticket which lasts 1, 2, 3 or 4 weeks and allows unlimited travel on the scheduled buses. Alternatively, there is a Full-Circle Passport which enables you to travel once (and only in one direction) round the ring road. Holders of these

tickets can obtain discounts on trips through the interior or on other services operated by the BSÍ.

Many visitors will want to travel through the interior and there are a number of scheduled services available during the summer months, but visitors who are in Iceland at either end of the tourist season should be aware that the interior may be closed then because of poor weather. The interior routes covered are: through Kjölur (which runs between Langjökull and Hofsjökull); through Sprengisandur (which runs between Hofsjökull and Vatnajökull); to Askja (which is to the north of Vatnajökull); through Fjallabak (which is to the northeast of Mýrdalsjökull); to Thórsmörk (which is to the north of Eyjafjallajökull); to Laki (which is to the north of Kirkjubæjarklaustur); to Veidivötn (the lakes to the north of Mýrdalsjökull); and to Kverkfjöll (which is at the northern edge of Vatnajökull).

Planes

The plane is to an Icelander what the train is to a European. Icelandair is the main internal airline and it operates through three companies: Flugleidir (based at Reykjavík), Flugfélag Nordurlands (based at Akureyri) and Flugfélag Austurlands (based at Egilsstadir).

The following places are connected by these three companies: Reykjavík, Akureyri, Bakkafjördur, Borgarfjördur eystri, Breiddalsvík, Egilsstadir, Grímsey, Höfn, Húsavik, Ísafjördur, Kópasker, Nordjördur, Ólafsfjördur, Patreksfjördur, Raufarhöfn, Saudárkrókur, Siglufjördur, Thingeyri, Thórshöfn, Vopnafjördur, Westman Islands (Heimaey).

Icelandair offer 'Air Rover' tickets which connect various towns and off-peak tickets for mid-week flights.

In addition to Icelandair, there are a number of small operators, like Ernir (based at Ísafjördur) and Mýflug, based at Mývatn, which operate services.

Ferries

Summer ferry services are given below. It is a wise precaution to book a berth a day or two ahead if your schedule is very tight or if it is a holiday weekend. 'Cars' indicates that vehicles are carried.

The *Akraborg* connects Reykjavík and Akranes (across Faxaflói); normally four per day; cars.

The *Baldur* connects Stykkishólmur and Brjánslækur across Breidafjördur (west coast); daily; cars.

The *Fagranes* connects Ísafjördur (in the Northwest Fjords) to various small islands and Hornstrandir; most days; cars.

The *Herjólfur* connects Thorlákshöfn to the Westman Islands (south coast); daily; cars.

The *Sæfari* connects Akureyri, Dalvík, Hrísey and Grímsey (all in Eyjafjördur); three days a week; no cars.

The *Sævar* connects Árskógssandur and Hrísey (in Eyjafjördur); daily; no cars.

Senior Citizens

Tour operators can usually suggest the tours that are best suited to senior citizens. These will usually be bus tours that are hotel-based.

Student and Youth Travel

There are discounts available on certain air fares but generally there are no special deals available for young people.

Telephones

Icelanders rely heavily on the telephone for communication – for obvious geographical reasons. Many Icelanders now have mobile phones. Consequently, the phone system is good and the telephone directory (*Simaskrá*) is excellent.

The telephone directory

The country is divided into eight regions with the codes (91) to (98); Reykjavík's is (91). The inside front cover of the directory gives a list of many settlements, together with their codes and the numbers of their emergency services. The directory then gives country codes (for telephoning abroad) and then starts the main lists of numbers; Reykjavík comes first. The other areas follow in the order of the codes and within each area the various settlements are listed separately in alphabetical order. Armed with this knowledge and a smattering of Icelandic, you can then find the addresses of people, bookshops, chemists, garages etc. Useful maps of various settlements are also given. A Yellow Pages section is

Walking in Skaftafell

at the back of the directory. One most intriguing aspect of the listings is that people's names are given in alphabetical order of their forenames, not their surnames. This means that you must know a person's first name before you have any chance of obtaining his/her number!

Telephoning Iceland from abroad

When telephoning Iceland, you will need to use four sets of digits: the international code, the code for Iceland, the area code within Iceland and the telephone number of the person or office you want to contact. The UK's international code is 010, the US and Canada's is 011 and Australia's is 0011. The code for Iceland is 354 from every country. The area code is the prefix, but the '9' is omitted.

Telephoning from Iceland

When telephoning abroad from Iceland, you will need to use four sets of digits: the international code, the code for the particular country, the area code within that country and the telephone number of the person or office you want to contact. The international code is 90. The UK's country code is 44, the US and Canada's is 1 and Australia's is 61. In case of difficulties, dial 08 for international enquiries and 09 for the international operator.

Telephone boxes

Public telephone boxes are seldom out-of-doors: the Post Office (*Póstur og Sími*) may be an exception. Cafés and hotels will usually have one. Dial 02 for the operator.

Most of the telephones are coin-operated but some, mainly in the Reykjavík area, use a magnetic card; these can be purchased in post offices. Telephones take 10 or 50 krónur coins, but not all phones can accept 50 krónur yet.

During office hours, you can use the telephones inside the post office; their great advantage is that you do not have to use coins, you just pay the cost of the call to the cashier.

Useful numbers

BSÍ bus station: (91) 22300/686464; **Icelandair** domestic booking and information: (91) 690200; international booking and information: (91) 690300/690100.

Time

Iceland follows Greenwich Mean Time throughout the year. During the summer it is one hour behind British Summer Time and four hours ahead of New York.

Tipping

There is no tipping in Iceland. In taxis you pay the fare shown on the meter.

Toilets

There are hardly any public toilets in the settlements so use the facilities in the roadside cafés, hotels, bus stations and campsites. In Reykjavík, the handiest toilet for the centre of the town is at the western end of Bankastræti, just before it meets Lækjartorg. Icelandic toilets are usually spotless, a relief even for wet and grubby tourists!

Tourist Offices

General tourist information can be obtained direct from the Iceland Tourist Board at Laugavegur 3, Reykjavík. However, they are not really in a position to answer detailed queries; ask a tour operator. The Iceland Tourist Board has an office in the US at 655 Third Avenue, New York, NY 10017.

Tourist Information Centres in Iceland

The main Tourist Information Centre in Iceland is in Reykjavík: it can supply a mass of leaflets and brochures about many parts of the country, and it also sells books and maps. The other offices are sometimes travel agents in particular settlements; the tourist industry is not large enough to make a distinction between the two types of service.

The Tourist Information Centres are:

Akranes: Hotel Ósk (tel: (93) 13314)

Akureyri: Umferðarmiðstöðinni, Hafnarstræti 82 (tel: (96)

27733/24442)
Blönduós: Hotel Blönduós (tel:
(95) 24126)
Egilsstadir: Ferdamidstöd
Austurlands, Kaupvangi 6 (tel:
(97) 12000)
Höfn: campsite (tel: (97) 81701)
Húsavík: Ferdaskrifstofa
Húsavíkur, Stóragardi 7 (tel: (96)
42100)
Hveragerdi: Ferdathjónusta
Sudurlands, Breidumörk 10 (tel:
(98) 34280)
Ísafjördur: Ferdaskrifstofa
Vestfjarda, Adalstræti 11 (tel:
(94) 3557)
Kirkjubæjarklaustur: community
centre (tel: (98) 74621)
Reykjavík: Bankastræti 2 (tel:
(91) 623045)
Saudárkrókur: Hotel Áning (tel:
(95) 36717)
Seydisfjördur: Austfar,
Fjardargata 8 (tel: (97) 21111)
Stadur: Stadurskali roadside
café (tel: (95) 11150)
Vík: campsite (tel: (98) 71345)

Tour Operators

Tour operators in Iceland

The following list gives a
selection of tour operators in
Reykjavik who cater for visitors
from abroad. They should be
able to organise almost anything
for you (except the weather!).
Atlantik Tours: Hallveigarstígur
1, Reykjavík. Tel: (91) 625066
BSÍ Travel Bureau: Central Bus
Station, Vatnsmýrarvegur,
Reykjavík. Tel: (91) 22300
Farfulgar, IYHF Travel:
Laufásvegur 41, Reykjavík. Tel:
(91) 24950 (youth hostels)
Ferðabær (Travel City):
Hafnarstræti 2, Reykjavík. Tel:
(91) 623020
Ferðaval Travel Bureau:
Lindargata 14, Reykjavík. Tel:

(91) 14480/12534
Gudmundur Jónasson Travel
Bureau: Borgartún 34, Reykjavík.
Tel: (91) 83222
Icelandic Highland Travel:
Lækjargata 3, Reykjavík. Tel:
(91) 22225/22220
Iceland Tourist Bureau:
Skógarhlíd 18, Reykjavík. Tel:
(91) 25855 (operators of the
Edda Hotels)
Reykjavík Excursions: Hotel
Loftleidir, Reykjavik Airport.
Tel: (91) 621011
Reykjavík Travel Bureau:
Adalstræti 16, Reykjavík. Tel:
(91) 621490
Sagaland Travel Bureau:
Bankastræti 2, Reykjavík. Tel:
(91) 627144
Saga Travel Bureau: Suðurgata
7, Reykjavík. Tel: (91) 624040
Samvinn Travel Bureau:
Austurstræti 12, Reykjavík. Tel:
(91) 691070/691010
Úrval-Útsyn/Iceland Access
Travel Bureau: Álfabakki 16,
Reykjavík. Tel: (91) 603060

Reykjavík harbour

Tour operators abroad

Iceland is an unusual tourist destination and your average travel agent at home will know little about the country. Because of this, it is quite essential to contact a specialist tour operator in your own country and deal through that firm. Names and addresses can be obtained through the Iceland Tourist Board or Icelandair. Then shop around for what suits you. A really knowledgeable tour operator can save you time and money in organising a really superb holiday.

Tours and Trips

Tours

One of the most popular ways of spending a holiday in Iceland is by going on a bus tour. Most of them start and finish in Reykjavík. This is an excellent way to see Iceland without all the hassle of driving or having to arrange transport and accommodation.

There are many tours available, ranging from those that involve camping each night to those that are hotel-based. There are also tours that cater for special interests such as walkers, bird-watchers and photographers. Tour operators should have details of these tours.

Many of the tours go through the interior and take in places where a visitor would be most unwise to travel without a four-wheel drive vehicle. Another major advantage of going on a touring holiday is that it should be quite possible to see many of the most popular tourist sites that are on the routes mentioned in the 'Planning an Itinerary' section.

Trips

Bus companies run trips and excursions from Reykjavík, Akureyri and many other centres. These offer a marvellous opportunity to travel relatively quickly to places such as Strokkur, Gullfoss or somewhere 'exotic' like Thórsmörk. Your tour operator should have details of these. Otherwise, enquire when you reach Iceland.

Once in Iceland, visitors find that Greenland is only another step away. A number of day trips are available to eastern and western Greenland. A fascinating place.

Walking

It's hard to avoid walking in Iceland, but for many, this is the purpose of their holiday. It is easy to see what attracts walkers: fascinating and diverse scenery, space, a lack of crowds and an unpolluted atmosphere. While there are

Time to stand and stare

undeniable difficulties and dangers that must be appreciated, experienced walkers will soon learn to cope with them as long as care is taken.

Since nearly all of the island is so uncrowded, there is no real need to seek out mountains or walking routes well away from so-called 'civilisation'; visitors will soon discover that there are fine walks just a few minutes away from nearly all the settlements. Remember that the greatest danger to walkers is isolation. If you twist your ankle in some out of the way spot then do not expect a casual passerby – at least not for several days! The best and safest attitude to adopt is to go to Iceland with no preconceptions about conquering great mountains – you will soon find out what kinds of terrain you are happiest walking on. When in the countryside, campsite wardens and hotel staff are always very helpful in suggesting interesting walks in the locality. You can also ask other visitors where they have been and when you are travelling on the road, look out for the places where the tour buses stop – there must be something interesting nearby! The Icelandic landscape can be very intimidating at times as there are vast open spaces where there is little or no shelter from wind and rain. In addition, overgrazing has drastically reduced plant-cover so that much of the land is dusty or gritty; frost action accentuates this and many surfaces are very soft and walking can be tiring. Hillsides can be very steep and

frost action has produced long scree slopes that are dangerous to walk up. Lavafields offer a number of difficulties. Block lava is very dangerous to cross as it is so jagged; it is also very slow work and exceptionally tiring. Moss may hide crevices into which a foot might slip. Glacial rivers flow quickly and are at their highest and most dangerous in the afternoon or after very warm weather.

Clothing
The Icelandic weather is somewhat unpredictable – visitors will soon discover that this is, at the very least, an understatement! It is quite possible to wake up to a temperature of over 25°C (77°F) and then shiver in a bitterly cold wind a couple of hours later. Wind- and waterproof clothing must be taken (jacket and leggings) and a warm jacket is essential. Gloves, woollen hat and a scarf are all needed too, as is warm underwear. Much of the terrain is very dusty and grit will get into your shoes, so a good pair of boots and thick socks are essential; gaiters may also be useful.

Denim trousers are very hard-wearing but notoriously absorbent, so they will soak up lots of rain and when the wind blows your legs can become dangerously cold. This is a very serious matter as the wind-chill factor is important. Remember that cold winds sweep down from the Arctic so north-facing hillsides in the north of the country can be particularly unpleasant, especially when conditions are wet.

LANGUAGE

The Icelandic language has its
roots in the ancient Germanic
languages and has changed little
since the Settlement, compared
to other languages of the same
family. Generally, it is related to
present-day Norwegian and
Faeroese.
It is a rather difficult language to
learn and there are a few special
letters which add to the
difficulties:
Special vowels: á, é, í, ó, ö, ú.
Other letters: æ, d, P, ý.
Note that P is often written as
th in English-language texts.
Some useful examples of
pronunciations are:
'a' as in man
'á' as in cow
'e' as in peach
'é' as in yet
'i' as in bit
'í' as in been
'o' as in hot
'ó' as in toe
'ö' as in burn
'u' as in earn
'ú' as in soon
'æ' as in I
'd' as in the
'P' as in thorn
Most of the Icelanders you will
meet in the tourist industry will
speak English. Many of them
will speak it very well,
especially if they have been
studying or working abroad.
However, it is best to know a
little Icelandic in order to be
able to read some signs and say
a few everyday words.

Accommodation
bathroom baðherbergi
bed rúm
bedroom svefnherbergi
campsite tjaldstædi
guesthouse gistihús
hotel hótel
bill reikningur
shower sturta
youth hostel farfuglaheimili

Conversation and notices
good day gódan daginn
goodbye bless
yes já
no nei
thank you takk fyrir
how much? hve mikid?
how many? hve mörg?
how far? hve langt?
left vinstri
right hægri
one way street einstefna
men karlar
women konur
not allowed bannað
push ýta
pull draga

Days
Sunday Sunnudagur
Monday Mánudagur
Tuesday Thridjudagur
Wednesday Midvikudagur
Thursday Fimmtudagur
Friday Föstudagur
Saturday Laugardagur

Documents
cheque ávísun
credit card kredit kort
customs tollur
driving licence ökuskirteini
passport vegabréf
travellers' cheques ferdatékkar
visa áritad vegabréf

Food and eating
beer bjór
bread braud
breakfast morgunmatur
butter smjör
cafétéria kaffiteria
coffee kaffi
evening meal kvöldmatur
menu matsedill

milk mjólk
restaurant veitingastadur
tea te
waiter thjónn

Numbers
zero núll
one einn
two tveir
three thrír
four fjórir
five fimm
six sex
seven sjö
eight átta
nine níu
10 tíu
11 ellefu
12 tólf
13 threttán
14 fjórtán
15 fimmtán
16 sextán
17 sautján
18 átján
19 nítján
20 tuttugu
30 thrjátíu
40 fjörutíu
50 fimmtíu
60 sextíu
70 sjötíu
80 áttatíu
90 níutíu
100 hundrad
1,000 thúsund

People and places
bank banki
bridge brú
church kirkja
community centre félagsheimili
doctor læknir
hospital spítali
house hús
information office
    upplýsingaskrifstofa
toilet salerni
museum safn
pharmacy apótek

school skóli
shop búd
supermarket stórmarkadur
swimming pool sundlaug

Transport
aeroplane flugvél
airport flugvöllur
bicycle hjól
boarding pass brottfarar spjald
bus straetisvagn
car bíll
car rental bilaleiga
car park bílastædi
coach rúta
diesel dísel
fare fargjald
ferry ferja
garage verkstædi
passenger farthegi
petrol bensín
ship skip
taxi leigubíll
ticket midi
timetable tímatafla

Catholic cathedral, Reykjavík

126

INDEX

INDEX

INDEX/ACKNOWLEDGEMENTS

The Automobile Association would like to thank the following photographers and libraries for their assistance in the preparation of this book.

All the pictures in this book are held in the DAVID WILLIAMS PICTURE LIBRARY except:

NATURE PHOTOGRAPHERS LTD 79 Redwing (R Tidman), 80 Yellow Marsh Saxifrage (A J Cleeve), 81 Red-necked phalarope (K J Carlson), 82 *Saxifraga Catyledon* (A J Cleeve), 83 Barrow's goldeneye (P R Sterry), 84 Slavonian grebe (P J Newman), 85 Seabird Cliffs Malariff (P R Sterry), 86 Black guillemot (P R Sterry).

GUNNAR SVEINSSON 99 Child, 101 National Day, 122 Walkers.